DOMINOES

Mansfield Park

LEVEL THREE 1000 HEADWORDS

OXFORD
UNIVERSITY PRESS

Great Clarendon Street, Oxford OX2 6DP

Oxford University Press is a department of the University of Oxford.
It furthers the University's objective of excellence in research, scholarship, and education by publishing worldwide in

Oxford New York

Auckland Cape Town Dar es Salaam Hong Kong Karachi Kuala Lumpur Madrid Melbourne Mexico City Nairobi New Delhi Shanghai Taipei Toronto

With offices in

Argentina Austria Brazil Chile Czech Republic France Greece Guatemala Hungary Italy Japan Poland Portugal Singapore South Korea Switzerland Thailand Turkey Ukraine Vietnam

OXFORD and OXFORD ENGLISH are registered trade marks of Oxford University Press in the UK and in certain other countries

First published in Dominoes 2010

2014 2013 2012 2011 2010

10 9 8 7 6 5 4 3 2 1

ISBN: 978 0 19 424828 0 Book
ISBN: 978 0 19 424786 3 Book and MultiROM Pack
MultiROM not available separately

Printed in China

ACKNOWLEDGEMENTS

Illustrations by: Fiona Sansom

The publisher would like to thank the following for permission to reproduce photographs: Alamy Images pp76 (Turkish boy in ceremonial costume/Vehbi Koca), 76 (Children dressed in ceremonial costumes/Ali Kabas), 82 (Cottesbrooke Hall, England/Tom Mackie); Corbis pp71 (Devon cottages/Philippa Lewis; Edifice), 74 (Coming of age ceremonies in Japan/Haruyoshi Yamaguchi); Getty Images p74 (Quinceanero celebration/AFP); Lonely Planet Images p76 (Children in traditional dress/Diego Lezama); Photolibrary pp57 (School children running from teacher/Blend Images), 74 (Girl receiving kiss at Quinceanera celebration/Corbis), 75 (Quinceanera cake decoration/Corbis), 75 (Teenage girl holding up shoe/Corbis); Reuters Pictures pp76 (Ceremony/Dimitar Dilkoff), 76 (Afghan woman carrying son/Zainal Abd Halim); Science and Society Picture Library pp42 (*The London to Birmingham Stage Coach*, 1801/ Science Museum Portal), 50 (Girl at a garden window, mid-late 19th century/Nigel Dobinson), 51 (HMS *Victory* at Portsmouth, c 1920s/NRM-Pictorial Collection), 63 (*Regent Quadrant, London*, c 1890/NMeM).

DOMINOES

Series Editors: Bill Bowler and Sue Parminter

Mansfield Park

Jane Austen

Text adaptation by Clare West

Illustrated by Fiona Sansom

Jane Austen (1775–1817) spent most of her life in Hampshire, in the south of England. Her life was quiet, she never married, and she lived happily with her family and friends. Her novels, including *Mansfield Park, Emma, Sense and Sensibility* and *Pride and Prejudice,* are some of the greatest novels in English. They have been adapted for film and television many times. *Emma* and *Mansfield Park* are both available as Domino titles.

OXFORD
UNIVERSITY PRESS

ACTIVITIES

BEFORE READING

1 Read about some of the characters from *Mansfield Park*. Complete the sentences about them below.

Sir Thomas and Lady Bertram live in a large country house called Mansfield Park. They have two sons, Edmund and Tom, and two daughters, Maria and Julia.

Lady Bertram has two sisters. Her older sister married a clergyman, and is called Mrs Norris.

Lady Bertram's other sister married an officer in the navy, and is called Mrs Price.

The Prices have a large family. One of their daughters, Fanny, comes to live at Mansfield Park. She misses her brother William very much.

a Sir Thomas Bertram is Fanny's ....

Fanny

b Tom is Fanny's .... and Edmund's ....

c Fanny is Mrs Norris's ....

d Lady Bertram is Fanny's ....

e Maria is Fanny's .... and Julia's ....

2 *Mansfield Park* is about these characters and their friends. What do you think happens to them in the story? Match each question with a character.

a Who falls ill and nearly dies?

b Who marries a rich man, and is miserable?

c Who falls in love with the wrong girl?

d Who runs away with an unsuitable man?

e Who marries a poor man, and is happy?

Chapter 1
A new home

About thirty years before our story begins, Miss Maria Ward – a young lady with only about £7,000 of her own – was lucky enough to **catch the eye** of a rich **baronet**. He was Sir Thomas Bertram of Mansfield Park, a large country house in Northamptonshire, about eighty miles north of London. He fell in love with her and married her, and she became Lady Bertram, with a fine house and plenty of money.

However, her two sisters, although pretty, did not manage to find husbands as good as hers. Sadly, there are more lovely women in the world than rich men to marry them. Her older sister married a poor **clergyman**, Mr Norris. Sir Thomas kindly offered Mr Norris the **living** of Mansfield, so Mr and Mrs Norris began their married life at the **Parsonage**, near the great house. The younger sister, Frances, chose an even worse husband, a young officer in the **navy**, and because she knew her sisters would not accept him in the family, she did not tell them until after her wedding. Lady Bertram, who preferred a quiet life, was too lazy to do anything much about it. But Mrs Norris could not rest until she had written a long letter to Frances, now Mrs Price, to tell her how stupid she had been. Mrs Price wrote back angrily, saying bitter things about Mrs Norris, Lady Bertram, and Sir Thomas – and his unnecessarily high **opinion** of himself. Mrs Norris felt unable to keep this reply to herself.

catch someone's eye (*past* **caught**) to be noticed by someone

baronet an important man from a rich family

clergyman a man who works for the church

living the work of a clergyman in a town or village, and the pay and the house that go with it

parsonage a country clergyman's house

navy a number of sailors who fight for their country

opinion what you think about someone or something

'How could Frances say those terrible things about you and dear Sir Thomas?' she said sadly to Lady Bertram. 'I knew her letter would make you both unhappy, but I felt it was my **duty** to inform you of it!' And from then on there was a cold silence for some years between Lady Bertram and Mrs Price, who lived many miles away and moved in very different **social** circles.

However, interestingly, Mrs Norris continued to hear from her younger sister, and almost every year she told the Bertrams, in an angry voice, 'Really, it's too bad of her! Frances has had another child!' By the end of eleven years, Mrs Price had a large family of eight children and would soon have a ninth. It seemed her husband was well enough to go drinking with his friends, but couldn't earn enough money to keep his family, and they were very poor. Now Mrs Price was sorry that she had **cut herself off from** her sisters, so she wrote a letter to Lady Bertram, asking for help.

duty what you must do to be a good person

social to do with meeting people

cut yourself off from (*past* **cut**) not to see or write to people in your family because you don't agree with them

Sir Thomas and Lady Bertram were happy to reply; they sent money and baby clothes. Often Mrs Norris said to Sir Thomas and Lady Bertram, when she visited them in the evenings, 'I wish we could do more for my poor sister! She has so many children, poor thing!' And soon she had an idea. 'Her oldest daughter is a girl of nine or so – why shouldn't we, the three of us, offer to take care of her? She could live with us at Mansfield. That would be a great help to poor Frances!'

Lady Bertram agreed at once, but Sir Thomas said seriously, 'If we take her away from her family, we must take care of her well, and that will cost quite a lot of money. And there are my sons to think of – I wouldn't want them to fall in love with the girl . . .'

Mrs Norris did not wait for him to finish. 'My dear Sir Thomas, I do understand you! Always so ready to think of other people! I completely agree with you. It may be expensive, but as I have no children of my own, I'll be only too pleased to help. And, you know, your sons will see her as their sister, so there'll be no danger there. Of course, I'll never love her as I love your own dear, dear children! But after all she is my poor sister's child, and I feel I must help her, as long as I have a bit of bread to give her.'

So it was agreed, and Mrs Norris wrote to Mrs Price, who accepted the offer. Sir Thomas was ready to pay for it all, while Mrs Norris, who talked so often about how kind and **generous** she was, was hoping to pay nothing. Her love of money was as great as her love of managing people, and she found saving her own money as easy as spending other people's.

The day before the little girl, whose name was Fanny Price, was **expected** to arrive, Sir Thomas was surprised to learn that Mrs Norris was unable to take the girl at the Parsonage. 'Poor Mr Norris is so ill at the moment,' she said, shaking her head sadly, 'that I'm very much afraid a child's noise would be bad for him. Of course,

generous always ready to give things to other people

expect to think that something will happen

when he gets better – if he gets better – I'll be happy to take care of her.'

So it was decided that Fanny Price would live at Mansfield Park, with her aunt and uncle, their two sons and two daughters. The sons, Edmund and Tom, were tall, good-looking young men of sixteen and seventeen, while the daughters, Maria and Julia, were beautiful, well-grown girls, only a year or two older than Fanny. They all had their own opinions, liked talking, and were much more sure of themselves than little Fanny. From the moment she arrived at the great house, so different from her parents' small one, she was afraid of everybody, ashamed of herself, and very unhappy. She missed her family, and could not say a word without crying. But she spoke so little that nobody noticed how miserable she was. Then one day Edmund, the younger son, found her sitting crying on the stairs.

'My dear little **cousin**,' he said gently, 'what can be the matter? Are you ill? How can I help you?'

'Nothing – no, thank you – it's very good of you all to have me here,' she whispered, still crying.

'You miss your family, I'm sure,' he said, smiling.

'Yes, I do, but most of all my brother William. He's the oldest in my family, you know, and my greatest friend. It's so hard to be away from him!' And poor little Fanny started crying all over again.

'He'll write to you, I'm sure,' said Edmund kindly.

'Yes, he promised to, but he told *me* to write first.'

'And when will you do that?'

She looked away from him and said unhappily, 'I don't know – I don't have any paper.'

'If that's the only problem, I can give you paper. Would it make you happy to write to William?'

'Yes, very.'

cousin the son (or daughter) of your father's (or mother's) brother (or sister)

'Well then, come with me to the breakfast room.'

He sat her down at a desk, and found some paper, and stayed with her while she wrote her letter. With his own hand he generously added his love to his cousin William, which pleased Fanny even more, and then he called a **servant** to take it to the post.

From this day on, Edmund's continued kindness to Fanny made her feel happier. The place became less strange to her, and the people there less frightening. She learnt to play with Maria and Julia, to read and talk to Edmund, and not to mind Aunt Norris too much. Mansfield Park became her home, and Edmund became her favourite person there; she loved him better than anybody in the world except her older brother William. But would her happiness last?

servant a person who works for someone rich

ACTIVITIES

READING CHECK

1 Put these sentences in the correct order. Number them 1–10.

- **a** Fanny is invited to live at Mansfield Park. ☐
- **b** Mrs Price asks Lady Bertram for help. ☐
- **c** Sir Thomas gives the Mansfield living to Mr Norris. [1]
- **d** Mrs Price and Mrs Norris write angry letters to each other. ☐
- **e** Mrs Norris has a bright idea about Fanny. ☐
- **f** Mr and Mrs Norris move to the Mansfield Parsonage. ☐
- **g** Fanny lives with the Bertrams, not Mrs Norris. ☐
- **h** Mrs Price has eight children in eleven years. ☐
- **i** Sir Thomas and Lady Bertram send money and baby clothes. ☐
- **j** Mrs Price tells her sisters that she is married. ☐

2 Are these sentences true or false? Tick the boxes.

	True	False
a Frances Price is proud of her husband.	☐	☑
b Lady Bertram is very lazy.	☐	☐
c Mrs Norris is kind and generous.	☐	☐
d The Price family don't have much money.	☐	☐
e Maria and Julia are quiet and unsure of themselves.	☐	☐
f Fanny is happy all the time at Mansfield Park.	☐	☐

WORD WORK

Find words in Chapter 1 to match the definitions.

- **a** a person who works in a rich person's house servant
- **b** the sailors who fight for their country _ _ _ _
- **c** a man who works for the church _ _ _ _ _ _ _ _ _
- **d** what you know is the right thing to do _ _ _ _
- **e** a gentleman from a rich, old family _ _ _ _ _ _ _
- **f** this describes someone who likes giving other people presents _ _ _ _ _ _ _ _
- **g** to be sure that certain things are going to happen _ _ _ _ _ _

ACTIVITIES

GUESS WHAT

What do you think happens in the next chapter? Match the names with the sentences. You may use the same name twice.

Sir Thomas	Maria	Fanny	Mrs Norris	Edmund	Julia

a .... moves to a smaller house.

b .... and .... have fun at a lot of parties.

c .... decides to marry.

d .... goes on a business trip.

e .... worries about Fanny's health.

f .... takes care of her aunt.

Chapter 2
Ideas of marriage

Five or six years after Fanny arrived at Mansfield Park, Mr Norris died, and Mrs Norris – now a **widow** – had to move from the Parsonage into another house in the village. A new clergyman, Dr Grant, took the living and moved into the empty Parsonage with his young wife. Sir Thomas thought it was a good time for Fanny to go and live with Mrs Norris. When Fanny heard about this, she was very unhappy. But there was no need for her to worry, because her aunt had no **intention** of giving her a home. Mrs Norris had been careful to choose a very small house. So when Lady Bertram asked about Fanny, Mrs Norris was able to reply, 'My dear sister! I'm an unhappy, helpless woman now – widowed, in poor health, and with only a little money to live on. I couldn't possibly have Fanny to live with me! And really, you know, I haven't a bed to give her, because I must keep a **spare room** for a friend.' No friends had ever come to stay at the Parsonage, but Mrs Norris now felt the need of a spare room for a friend very strongly.

So, to her great **delight**, Fanny stayed at Mansfield Park, and life went on as pleasantly as before.

About a year later, Sir Thomas began to worry about his business interests in Antigua, in the West Indies. So he decided to travel there to find out what was happening. It was his intention to go on the journey with his oldest son, Tom, to take him away from the circle of careless friends with whom he usually spent most of his time and lots of the family's money. They would be away for nearly twelve months.

The Miss Bertrams were not sorry to see their father go. They felt that they were now free to enjoy themselves. That autumn and winter they were invited to all the parties and **balls** in the country

widow a woman whose husband is dead

intention a plan or idea

spare room a room in a house where visitors stay

delight happiness

ball a formal party with dancing

towns around them, and were very popular with the young men. Lady Bertram was too lazy to go with her daughters, but luckily Mrs Norris was happy to take her sister's place. Fanny was not invited by anybody – she did not expect it – but she made herself very useful to Lady Bertram while the rest of the family were out. She enjoyed the quiet evenings by the fire, listening to her aunt and reading to her. Then when her cousins returned, she loved to hear all about the parties and the balls. 'Who did Edmund dance with?' was the first question that she always asked.

In the spring, Edmund noticed that Fanny was not looking well. He decided that she was spending too much time indoors. So he bought a new horse for her to use, and after that Fanny rode out every morning. She was delighted with the horse, but even more delighted with Edmund's kindness. She could not find the words to tell him how grateful she was.

By now Mrs Norris had managed to introduce her favourite **niece**, Maria, to Mr Rushworth – one of the richest young men in the country. He was not very intelligent and was no good at making conversation, but he looked pleasant enough. He had seen the beautiful Maria, and thought he was in love. Maria, who was

niece your sister's (or brother's) daughter

almost twenty-one, was beginning to think that it was time to marry. As Mrs Rushworth, she would have a larger **income** than her father, as well as a town house in London. So she felt that it was her duty to marry Mr Rushworth if she could.

Mrs Norris did her best to help things along. 'How delightful it will be to see dear Maria well married!' she thought. 'And how grateful dear Sir Thomas and Lady Bertram will be to me!'

Soon Maria and Mr Rushworth were **engaged**, to the delight of both their families. Edmund was the only one who did not like his sister's future husband. He often said to himself, 'If Rushworth didn't have an income of twelve thousand a year, we'd all think him very stupid!'

When Tom arrived home from Antigua soon afterwards, he brought with him a letter from Sir Thomas. The letter gave Sir Thomas's **consent** to Maria's **choice** of husband, asking only that Maria and Mr Rushworth should not marry until he returned home in the summer.

In July, when Fanny had just had her eighteenth birthday, two new people – Henry and Mary Crawford – arrived in the village. Because they were the younger brother and sister of Mrs Grant, the new clergyman's wife, they came to stay at the Parsonage for a time. Henry owned a large house and land in another part of the country, while Mary had an income of £20,000 a year. Mary was very pretty, and her brother was really **charming**.

Mrs Grant had a plan which she discussed with her sister, Mary. 'Who could be a better husband for you than Tom Bertram, Sir Thomas's oldest son?'

Mary liked the idea very much, although she pretended to laugh at her sister's choice.

'And then,' added Mrs Grant, 'I'd like Henry to marry Julia, the younger Miss Bertram. She'll make him very happy, I'm sure.'

income money that you get every month, or every year, from work, family or land

engaged when two people agree that they are going to marry

consent when somebody agrees to something

choice when you choose something

charming nice to other people

'My dear sister,' said Mary, smiling, 'if you can **persuade** Henry to think of **marriage**, you are cleverer than half the women in England. He has broken so many hearts!'

The Miss Bertrams liked Mary Crawford at once, and they liked her brother even more. Before Henry had been at Mansfield a week, Julia was ready for him to fall in love with her. And Maria, although she was engaged, clearly enjoyed spending time with him. Henry himself did not want them to 'die of love', but he just could not keep away from these two beautiful girls. He persuaded himself that they could take care of themselves well enough when they were with him.

Mary Crawford soon decided that Mrs Grant's plan for her was a sensible one. Both Edmund and Tom were fine-looking men, but she felt she liked the oldest son best. It was no surprise to her – she often *did* prefer the oldest son in a family. When Tom's father died, the young man would become Sir Thomas, a baronet with his own country house and gardens, and a large income. She thought she would consent to marry him. But in a few days he was leaving Mansfield to spend time with some friends at the horse **races**. Perhaps before he left he would ask her to be his wife.

persuade to make somebody change their way of thinking by speaking to them

marriage when two people are married

race when horses run and the fastest horse wins

READING CHECK

Tick the boxes to complete the sentences.

a Mrs Norris leaves the Parsonage because …
- **1** she has argued with Sir Thomas. ☐
- **2** the house is too big for her. ☐
- **3** a new clergyman has to move in. ☑

b Mrs Norris wants to …
- **1** have Fanny to live with her. ☐
- **2** spend as little money as possible. ☐
- **3** invite several friends to stay. ☐

c Sir Thomas travels to the West Indies in order to …
- **1** have a good holiday. ☐
- **2** show Tom some interesting places. ☐
- **3** take care of his business interests. ☐

d While Sir Thomas is away, Fanny enjoys …
- **1** staying at home with Lady Bertram. ☐
- **2** going to balls with her cousins. ☐
- **3** dancing with Edmund. ☐

e Maria decides to marry Mr Rushworth because …
- **1** she loves him. ☐
- **2** he's very rich. ☐
- **3** he cleverly persuades her. ☐

f Mary Crawford would like to marry Tom Bertram because …
- **1** he's already in love with her. ☐
- **2** he'll be a baronet one day. ☐
- **3** he's better-looking than Edmund. ☐

ACTIVITIES

WORD WORK

Correct the boxed words in these sentences.

a Mrs Norris has become a [window]. ..widow..
b She has no [square] room for Fanny. ....
c Maria is Mrs Norris's favourite [piece]. ....
d The Miss Bertrams like dancing at [walls]. ....
e Sir Thomas sends a letter of [content] from Antigua. ....
f Henry Crawford is a very [harming] man. ....

Find words in the dancing shoes to complete the sentences.

a

b

c

d

e

f

a Mrs Norris has no intention... of taking care of Fanny.
b To Fanny's d.................., she is allowed to stay at Mansfield Park.
c Maria and Mr Rushworth become e.................. .
d Edmund does not like Maria's c.................. of husband.
e Mrs Grant hopes to p.................. Henry to marry.
f Mary Crawford has a good i.................. of her own.

GUESS WHAT

What do you think happens in the next chapter? Match the characters with the sentences. You may use the names twice.

a .... learns how to ride.
b .... gets angry with Mrs Norris.
c .... shows how stupid he is.
d .... lends a horse to someone.
e .... visits the Parsonage every day.
f .... feels ill because of the heat.

Fanny

Edmund

Mr Rushworth

Mary Crawford

Chapter 3
Falling in love

When Tom Bertram left Mansfield for the horse races, he had still not said anything about marrying anyone. Mary Crawford felt sure she would miss his good-looking face and amusing conversation. That evening the Grants and the Crawfords were invited to dinner at Mansfield Park. Mr Rushworth, Maria's **fiancé**, was also there, for the first time since the Crawfords' arrival. He had recently returned from a visit to a friend's house, and could not stop talking about it.

'I wish you could see it!' he said. 'I never saw a place so changed in all my life! I think that *now* the gardens are some of the finest in the country! When I got back to *my* house – Sotherton Court, you know – I felt very low. It looked just like a prison, a miserable old prison!'

'Oh really, Mr Rushworth!' cried Mrs Norris. 'Sotherton Court is far from a prison! It's the most wonderful old place in the world!'

Mr Rushworth shook his head sadly. 'Smith – that's my friend, you know – had a man called Repton to help him plan all the changes. I think I'd better have him to help *me* at Sotherton. He costs five **guineas** a day.'

'How right you are!' cried Mrs Norris. 'An excellent choice! And what is five guineas daily after all? I always say the cost doesn't matter, if the man really knows his job!'

'Smith's place is so much better than before,' Mr Rushworth continued. 'Everyone says so. I think I shall have Repton.'

'Mr Rushworth can do as he pleases, of course,' said Edmund politely, 'but I think I'd prefer to make my own mistakes and plan my garden myself.'

Mary Crawford listened. 'What a stupid man Mr Rushworth is!' she thought. 'But Edmund is so sensible!'

fiancé the man that a woman is going to marry

guinea an old British gold coin worth just over a pound (about £1.05)

'Mr Bertram,' she said, turning brightly towards Edmund, 'I have news of my **harp**. It has arrived safely at Northampton. And tomorrow Henry, who is always so generous and kind, is going to fetch it for me.'

'The harp is my favourite **instrument**, Miss Crawford,' Edmund replied. 'I hope you will soon let me hear you play.'

'I've never heard the harp at all,' said Fanny. 'I would love to hear it too.'

'I shall be most happy to play for you both,' replied Mary with a charming smile. And so the evening ended.

The next morning Edmund asked Fanny **eagerly**, 'What do you think of Miss Crawford?'

'I like her very much. She talks amusingly, and she's so pretty!'

'Yes, what a lovely face! What intelligent conversation!'

It was clear that Edmund **admired** Mary Crawford greatly, and in the next few days his **admiration** for her grew still greater. The harp arrived, and he went every day to the Parsonage to hear his favourite instrument played beautifully. A pretty, clever young woman like Mary Crawford – playing a harp as fine-looking as herself, near a door opening on to a garden in summer – was enough to catch any man's heart.

harp you make music on this instrument by pulling the strings with your fingers

instrument you play music on this

eagerly in a very interested way

admire to think that somebody (or something) is very good

admiration a feeling of liking someone (or something) very much

flatter to say nice things to someone because you want to please him or her

opportunity a time when you can do something that was not possible before

exercise something that you do which keeps your body healthy

sofa a long soft seat for people to sit on together

sewing to join or fix pieces of cloth together to make things

headache a pain in the head

Mary realized to her surprise that she had begun to look forward to Edmund's visits. She did not know why, because he was only a younger son and he did not try to **flatter** her. But she liked to have him near her; that was enough.

Fanny did not wonder that Edmund visited the Parsonage every day; she was sorry that she herself did not see him so often now. But she did feel hurt when Edmund asked if Miss Crawford could borrow her horse – the horse which he himself had generously bought for her to use! Mary had decided to learn to ride, and Edmund wished to teach her. Fanny gave her consent, but she knew this was an **opportunity** for Edmund and Miss Crawford to spend even more time together.

At first, Edmund began with good intentions. He kept Miss Crawford's riding lessons short, so that he could return the horse to Fanny for her daily **exercise**. But soon Mary Crawford wanted to ride for a longer time, and for the next four days the Miss Bertrams, the Grants, the Crawfords and Edmund rode round the countryside all day. The weather was very hot, but the riders were able to keep cool by keeping under the trees and out of the sun, and they greatly enjoyed themselves.

When Edmund returned to Mansfield Park one very warm evening, he looked round the sitting room and said, 'Where's Fanny?'

'I'm here,' called a soft voice from a dark corner at the other end of the room where she was sitting on the **sofa**.

'What are you doing over there on the sofa, Fanny, you lazy girl?' said Mrs Norris crossly. 'Come and do some **sewing** at the table with us. You should learn to think of your duty to other people.'

Before she had finished speaking, Fanny was at the table, working at her sewing. Edmund looked closely at her.

'Fanny,' he said, 'I'm sure you have a **headache**.'

'Well, yes, Edmund, but it's not very bad, really.'

'Did you go out today, when it was so hot?'

'Indeed she did, Edmund,' said Lady Bertram. 'She was cutting flowers for me in the garden. And then she had to walk twice to the village and back, for Mrs Norris.'

'What!' cried Edmund. 'Walking as well as cutting flowers? In this heat? Of course she has a headache!'

'Fanny should take more exercise,' said Mrs Norris angrily. 'She hasn't been riding for four days now. And if she doesn't ride, she should walk.'

'She is not as strong as you are, **ma'am**,' replied Edmund. He said no more, but brought a glass of **wine** to Fanny, and made her drink most of it, as a medicine, to bring the colour back to her face. He was angry with his mother and aunt, but still angrier with himself. He was ashamed to think that for four days she had not been able to take her usual exercise, because he had thought only of Miss Crawford's wishes.

Fanny went quietly upstairs to bed. In her dark corner of the sitting room, the ache in her heart had been much greater than the ache in her head. Now Edmund's kindness in bringing her that wine had made her so happy that she could not think very clearly.

ma'am a polite way of speaking to a rich or important woman

wine a red or white alcoholic drink made from grapes

ACTIVITIES

READING CHECK

What do they say? Complete the sentences.

1. You should learn to think of your duty to other people.
2. I've never heard the harp at all.
3. She is not as strong as you are, ma'am.
4. What a lovely face! What intelligent conversation!
5. It looked just like a prison.
6. I shall be most happy to play for you both.
7. She was cutting flowers for me in the garden.

a Mr Rushworth says about his house, '*It looked just like a prison!*'

b '...,' Fanny says to Edmund and Mary.

c Mary says to Edmund and Fanny, '...'

d Edmund says about Mary: '...'

e Mrs Norris says to Fanny, '...'

f '...,' Lady Bertram says about Fanny.

g '...,' Edmund tells Mrs Norris about Fanny.

WORD WORK

Find words from Chapter 3 in the crossword by completing the sentences on page 19.

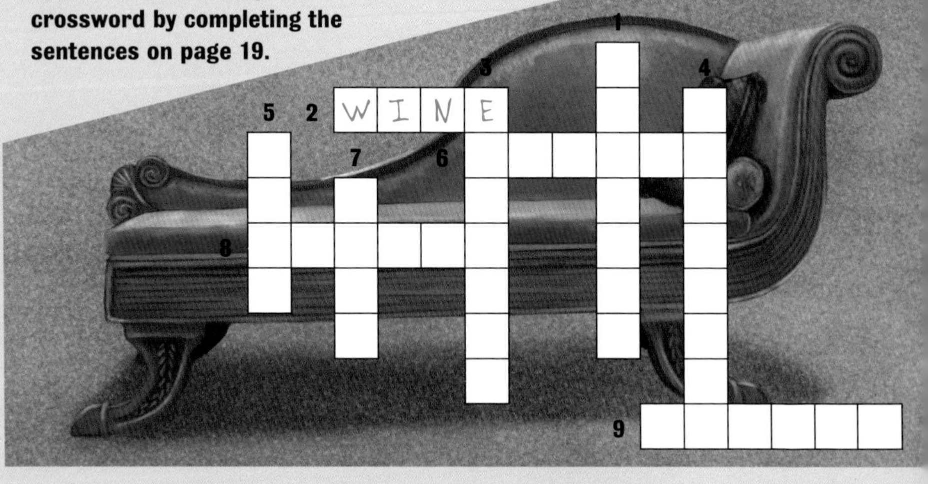

Across

2 Edmund brings Fanny a glass of ...wine.... to drink, but we don't know if it's red or white.

6 Edmund begins to .... Mary Crawford very much. That's to say, he thinks very highly of her.

8 Mr Rushworth has agreed to marry Maria. So he is her ....

9 The ladies do their .... – making and mending clothes – together at the table.

Down

1 The garden designer, Mr Repton, is paid five .... a day. That makes twenty one pounds for four days' work.

3 Edmund .... asks what Fanny thinks of Mary Crawford. He is very interested in hearing his cousin's ideas.

4 Fanny sometimes has a bad .... , and then she must rest her head and go to bed.

5 The .... – where two people can sit together – is in a dark corner of the sitting room.

7 Mary Crawford plays the .... beautifully. Her fingers move backwards and forwards to pull the strings very cleverly.

GUESS WHAT

Make five sentences with these phrases to find out what happens in the next chapter.

a Edmund wants to	**1** spend some time	**i** for everybody.
b Mary discovers that	**2** is not a happy time	**ii** be a clergyman.
c Maria and Henry manage to	**3** make sure that Fanny	**iii** Edmund likes Mary very much.
d Fanny has to	**4** accept the fact that	**iv** alone together.
e The visit to Sotherton	**5** Edmund is going to	**v** has a day out.

Chapter 4
A visit to Sotherton

Fanny was out riding the next day when Mr Rushworth and his mother arrived. They came to invite the Bertrams and the Crawfords to visit Sotherton Court. Mr Rushworth hoped they would give him ideas for **improving** his gardens.

Mrs Norris was very excited. 'We shall be delighted to accept, my dear Mrs Rushworth,' she said eagerly. 'Our two dear girls, Edmund and myself, that is. Lady Bertram cannot come – she gets tired so easily. But Fanny will stay and be her **companion**.'

Edmund turned to his mother. 'I don't suppose, ma'am, that you wish to stop Fanny enjoying herself?' he asked.

'Well, no,' replied Lady Bertram slowly, 'but I need her at home with me.'

'You won't need her if *I* stay with you. I know Fanny would really like to see Sotherton, and she doesn't often get what she wants.'

Mrs Norris was very cross at this change to her plan. But luckily Mrs Grant offered to be Lady Bertram's companion for the day, so Edmund could join the party.

On the day of the visit, the Miss Bertrams, Mrs Norris, Miss Crawford and Fanny were driven by Henry Crawford in his **carriage**, while Edmund rode his horse to Sotherton. Fanny was very happy to look silently out of the carriage windows at the beautiful countryside. She was not like Mary Crawford, whose only interest was in people, and who preferred talking. But they were like each other in one way – they both kept their eyes on the road, looking out for Edmund; and when they saw his horse, both of them cried 'There he is!' at the same moment.

Mr Rushworth welcomed his **guests** to Sotherton. They ate a light meal, and then Mrs Rushworth showed them round the many

improve to make something better

companion a person who spends a lot of time with someone

carriage an old kind of car that horses pull

guest a person that you invite to your home

rooms of the house. Finally they reached the old **chapel**.

'The family and servants used to say their **prayers** here in the past,' said Mrs Rushworth. 'But my husband decided it wasn't necessary to continue with this.'

'That was an **improvement**,' said Miss Crawford, with a smile, to Edmund.

'Well, I'm sorry it was stopped!' cried Fanny bravely. 'It's a fine thing when a whole family says their prayers together!'

'Very fine, indeed!' said Miss Crawford, laughing. 'Just think how the daughters of the family hated getting up early and saying their prayers in this cold chapel. I'm sure they had no choice in the matter. And I don't suppose the poor clergyman was even worth looking at!'

There was a short silence. Fanny reddened, and felt too angry to speak. Edmund was just going to reply, when Julia called to them.

'Do look at Mr Rushworth and Maria! They're standing side by side in front of the **altar** – all ready for their wedding!'

chapel a room in a house that is used as a church

prayer when people speak to God

improvement when you make something better

altar a high table in a church or chapel; people are married in front of it

Henry Crawford had noticed this, too. He went closer to Maria and said, in a voice which only she could hear, 'I don't like to see you so near the altar.' She whispered a reply to him.

Julia continued, 'How unlucky that you **aren't ordained** yet, Edmund! You could marry them here and now!'

Miss Crawford's face lost all its colour when she heard this.

'Ordained!' she said to Edmund. 'What, are you going to be a clergyman?'

'Yes, soon after my father returns from Antigua.'

'I'm sorry I spoke of clergymen with so little **respect**.'

By now they all seemed to feel they had been in the chapel long enough, and decided to go out into the gardens.

Henry Crawford, Maria and Mr Rushworth started discussing possible improvements in the flower garden, while Miss Crawford, Edmund and Fanny walked towards a small wood. Mrs Rushworth and Mrs Norris walked more slowly behind them all, and poor Julia had to walk with these older ladies. She wanted so much to escape to the flower garden!

Miss Crawford said to Edmund, 'I'm surprised that you're going to be a clergyman, Mr Bertram.'

'Why are you surprised, Miss Crawford?'

'Because as a clergyman you will never be rich or well-known in the world. A clergyman is nothing.'

be ordained to become a priest or clergyman

respect when you are careful of someone's feelings because you admire them

'*I* think a clergyman has an important job to do. Helping people see what's right and what's wrong – would you call that nothing?'

'Come, change your plans, Mr Bertram. It's not too late. You really could do something better.'

'I'm afraid you can't persuade me, Miss Crawford.'

There was a silence. After a moment, Fanny said gently, 'If you don't mind, I'd like to sit down when we come to a seat.'

'My dear Fanny,' cried Edmund, taking her arm at once, 'I'm so thoughtless! I hope you aren't *very* tired. Would you take my other arm, Miss Crawford?'

The three of them walked on to the next seat, where Fanny sat down to rest. But Edmund and Mary Crawford wanted more exercise. So they walked on into the wood, promising to return very soon.

Twenty minutes passed. Then Maria, her fiancé and Henry Crawford came up to Fanny's seat. Nearby there was a **gate** into the park, but it was locked. Maria and Henry were eager to enter the park, and they persuaded Mr Rushworth to return to the house to fetch the key. While he was away, they managed to push their way round the side of the gate, and walked quickly off together into the park. Fanny was surprised at their bad **behaviour**.

When Mr Rushworth came back with the key to the gate, he was very cross to discover that Maria and Henry had not waited for him. He hurried after them into the park, leaving Fanny alone again.

Finally she decided to go and search for Edmund and Miss Crawford. She found them sitting happily under a tree, and realized sadly that Edmund had not missed her at all.

Soon it was time for everyone to return to the house for dinner. Conversation seemed a little difficult; only Maria Bertram and Henry Crawford had plenty to say. And on the way home in the evening, there was silence in the carriage, as Mr Rushworth's guests thought long and hard about their day.

gate an outside door into a garden

behaviour the way that you do and say things

READING CHECK

Correct ten more mistakes in the chapter summary.

Mr Rushworth and his ~~father~~ mother invite the Bertrams and the Grants to come to visit their large town house, Sotherton Court. Lady Bertram is happy to accept the invitation, and everyone looks forward to the visit. When they arrive at Sotherton, they all eat a large meal, and then the Rushworths show them round the house. Next, they all go out into the fields, for some fresh air. Julia wants to argue with Henry, but she has to stay with the younger women. So Maria makes the most of her opportunity and escapes from her brother, hurrying into the park with Henry. While this is happening, Mary Crawford makes it clear to Edmund that she wants to marry a man who is both intelligent and famous. Edmund doesn't worry about this; he still thinks she is charming. Fanny realizes how he feels, and so she is very happy as the families drive home to Mansfield.

WORD WORK

1 Find words in the garden to complete the sentences.

a Because Lady Bertram doesn't like to be alone, Mrs Grant offers to be her companion.

b Mr Rushworth welcomes his .... to his house when they first arrive.

c In the past, the Rushworths and their servants said .... in church together.

d Edmund is going to be .... and become a clergyman soon.

e Mr Rushworth wants to .... his gardens because he thinks that they aren't fashionable.

f Mary Crawford shows no .... for clergymen. She laughs at them.

g Edmund's .... makes Fanny sad. She doesn't like what he does.

These words don't match the pictures. Correct them.

a ~~carriage~~ ...altar...

b chapel ....

c altar ....

d gate ....

GUESS WHAT

Match the first and second parts of these sentences to find out what happens in the next chapter.

a Maria is sorry to hear that ....
b Mary tries to persuade Edmund ....
c Fanny warns Edmund ....
d A visitor has an idea, ...
e Edmund tries to stop his sisters ....
f Edmund changes his opinion, ...
g Fanny worries about ....

1 which Tom likes very much.
2 and agrees to do some acting.
3 behaving badly.
4 about Henry's character.
5 to go into the army or navy.
6 what will happen next.
7 Sir Thomas is coming home soon.

Chapter 5
The play

Several days after the visit to Sotherton, a letter from Sir Thomas in Antigua reached Mansfield Park. The Miss Bertrams were sorry to learn from it that their father would be home soon. November was the black month fixed for his return. Julia would no longer be free to go to parties when she wished. And Maria, poor Maria! When her father returned, she would have to marry the man she had chosen as her husband, Mr Rushworth. She could not **bear** to think of it.

'November is three months away,' she said to herself hopefully. 'Anything could happen between now and then.'

Miss Crawford heard the news that evening at Mansfield Park.

'How happy Mr Rushworth looks today!' she said to Edmund. 'He's looking forward to November. But I can't help thinking, Mr Bertram, that your sister is **sacrificing herself**, to marry him.'

'Not at all,' replied Edmund with a serious smile. 'She decided to accept him herself.'

'Oh yes, I know, I was just **joking**. She's doing what any young woman would do, and I'm sure she'll be very happy. But what about you, Mr Bertram? Are *you* sacrificing yourself?'

'You mean, by being ordained? I can promise you, no one has persuaded me to do it. It's my own wish.'

'It's lucky, isn't it, that your father has a good living ready for you, which you'll be able to take?'

'I suppose you think *that* has **influenced** my choice.'

bear to be able to accept and live with something unpleasant

sacrifice yourself to agree to do something that you don't want to do

joke to say something funny

influence to change someone by words or behaviour; when you change someone by words or behaviour

'I'm sure it hasn't!' cried Fanny, who was listening to their conversation.

'Thank you for thinking well of me, Fanny, but perhaps it did influence me a little. I don't think that's wrong. A man can still be a good clergyman – it doesn't matter if he has a comfortable income.'

'But why not go into the army or the navy?' asked Mary Crawford eagerly. 'You'd live the exciting, dangerous life of a brave officer, people would invite you to all the fashionable parties. What kind of life is a clergyman's? He just reads the newspaper, watches the weather, and **quarrels** with his wife. The only thing he's really interested in is his dinner.'

'Do you know any clergymen like that, Miss Crawford?'

'I do. My sister's husband, Dr Grant, is most kind to me, but I'm afraid he's just like the clergyman I've described to you. My poor sister! How can she bear it?'

'I *am* sorry to hear that,' Edmund replied. 'Fanny, what can we say? How can we persuade Miss Crawford to agree with us?'

'Dr Grant is still an excellent clergyman, even if he is sometimes a little cross,' said Fanny. 'There are many army and navy officers, I'm sure, who enjoy their food and argue with their wives.'

'Well, Miss Price,' said Mary Crawford, laughing, 'I hope you never marry a clergyman who quarrels with you every day!'

'There's no man alive who could often quarrel with Fanny,' said Edmund, smiling kindly at his cousin.

Just then Miss Crawford was called by the Miss Bertrams to play the **piano** for them. As Mary walked over to the instrument, Edmund's eyes followed her in admiration.

'How well she walks!' he said to Fanny. 'How amusing and charming she is! How generously she gives her time to others!'

Fanny felt she had to agree. Edmund stood next to her for a short while, but he kept looking towards the ladies at the other end of the

quarrel to argue angrily with someone

piano a big musical instrument that you play by pressing black and white keys

room. Soon he too went to join his sisters round the piano. Fanny was left alone, looking sadly out of the window at the stars in the sky.

In August, Tom Bertram arrived home again. He was as good-looking as ever, but Mary Crawford realized she was no longer interested in him. 'It's stupid of me, of course,' she thought crossly, 'but I really don't want to marry him now – although he'll be a baronet one day!'

Henry Crawford often visited Mansfield Park, where he spent as much time with Maria as with Julia. Both young women were flattered, and each thought she was his favourite. Fanny was worried by this behaviour, and spoke to Edmund about it. But he told her there was no danger of Maria falling in love with Mr Crawford, because she was engaged to Mr Rushworth. 'Don't worry about it, Fanny,' Edmund added. So Fanny tried hard not to think about it any more.

A friend of Tom Bertram's, called John Yates, came to stay for a few days at Mansfield Park. He was a fashionable young man, who had nothing to do except spend his father's money. At a house where he had recently stayed, the family and their guests had acted in a **play**. Yates had enjoyed this very much, and now **suggested** that they should do the same at Mansfield Park. The young people accepted his idea with delight. Tom Bertram, as the head of the family while Sir Thomas was away, offered the use of any room in the house.

But Edmund did not like the plan at all, and later he spoke quietly to Tom about it. 'Surely, Tom, you can't want to amuse yourself by acting, when our father is away on a dangerous journey? And what about Maria? We must be careful of her good name. She's engaged to Mr Rushworth, and shouldn't be alone with any other unmarried men.'

'You're so serious, Edmund!' laughed Tom. 'It's just a bit of fun.

play a piece of writing that people act in a theatre

suggest to say that something is a good idea

Rushworth himself is making no difficulty about it.'

'I know our father wouldn't like it,' Edmund said.

'I know him as well as you do, Edmund. Take care of your own business, and I'll take care of the rest of the family. Don't act yourself, but don't expect to decide for other people.'

'I have no intention of acting myself.'

Tom walked out of the room. Fanny, who had heard it all, and who agreed with Edmund, said to him, 'Perhaps you can use your influence with the others, to stop it happening.'

But Edmund was not hopeful. The next day he tried to persuade his sisters that it was a bad idea, but both were eagerly looking forward to acting in the play. Lady Bertram did not mind what her children and guests did, as long as they did not wake her from her afternoon sleep. Mrs Norris was pleased that she was needed to help with the **costumes**. Henry and Mary Crawford also wanted to act in the play. None of them could understand what Edmund was worrying about.

Soon the group of actors had chosen a play called *Lovers' Promises*. Maria took the **part** of the beautiful Agatha, an unmarried woman with a secret love in her past, and Henry Crawford took the part of Frederick, Agatha's clever only son who wants to help her meet and marry her old lover. These two started **rehearsing** at once, and for the next few days were often seen whispering together in quiet corners of the house. Other parts were discussed and finally accepted. Even Fanny was offered a small part, but she knew she would hate acting, and refused.

Mary Crawford took the part of Amelia, another beautiful woman in the play. But there was a problem. Who would act the part of her lover, a clergyman called Anhalt? Edmund was asked, but he refused. So Tom suggested inviting a young man who lived in the next village to be Anhalt.

costume the clothes that an actor wears in a play

part one of the characters in a play

rehearse to practise a play

That evening Edmund came to find Fanny. 'This acting gets worse and worse,' he said. 'What an unsuitable play they've chosen! It's all about love and lovers! And now they're going to bring in a stranger to act with my sisters and Miss Crawford!'

'But what can we do?' Fanny asked.

'There is only one thing to do. *I* must take the part of Anhalt, and then Miss Crawford won't have to act with a stranger. What do you think, Fanny?'

stage a high platform which is made of wood where people stand when they act a play

scene a part of a play that happens at one time in one place

Fanny did not know what to say. 'I'm sure she will be very pleased–' she began.

'There! I knew you'd agree with me! Thank you, dear Fanny. I'll go and tell the others at once.' And before Fanny could tell him her real opinion, he hurried eagerly out of the room.

'How strong Miss Crawford's influence on him is!' thought Fanny miserably. 'He will do anything for her!'

For the next few days the house was full of noise and people. Workmen came to build a **stage** in Sir Thomas's library, and servants ran here and there to obey Tom's orders. The actors rehearsed morning and evening, and Fanny helped Mrs Norris with the sewing of the costumes.

The worst moment for Fanny came when Edmund and Miss Crawford asked her to help them rehearse their love **scene**. At first she felt flattered to be of help, but soon she saw the way they looked at each other as they spoke their words. 'It's only a play!' she told herself. 'But oh! I don't think they're acting!' And that night she cried herself to sleep in her small bedroom.

The next evening there was going to be a full rehearsal in costume, in front of Lady Bertram, Mrs Norris, the Grants and Fanny. They were all waiting for the play to begin, when suddenly Julia ran into the room.

'Our father is here!' she cried. 'He's in the hall at this moment!'

READING CHECK

Tick the correct answers.

a Why is Maria unhappy to hear that her father is returning?

1 She is sorry that she has behaved badly. ☐

2 She is worried that his journey is dangerous. ☐

3 She doesn't want to marry her fiancé. ☑

b Why does Mary describe a clergyman's life as boring and useless?

1 To make conversation. ☐

2 To change Edmund's plans. ☐

3 To persuade Fanny that she is right. ☐

c What does Edmund think about Fanny?

1 She's a good, sweet girl. ☐

2 She's amusing and charming. ☐

3 She's beautiful and intelligent. ☐

d Why doesn't Fanny's warning worry Edmund?

1 He knows that Julia isn't in love. ☐

2 He thinks that Henry is a gentleman. ☐

3 He's sure that Maria won't break her engagement. ☐

e Why do Tom and Edmund quarrel?

1 They don't agree about Yates's suggestion. ☐

2 They are unable to be honest with each other. ☐

3 They don't understand their sisters' wishes. ☐

f How does Fanny feel about Edmund and Mary?

1 She's angry about their behaviour. ☐

2 She's afraid that they love each other. ☐

3 She's ashamed of the influence they have on her. ☐

WORD WORK

Find words in the cloak to complete the sentences.

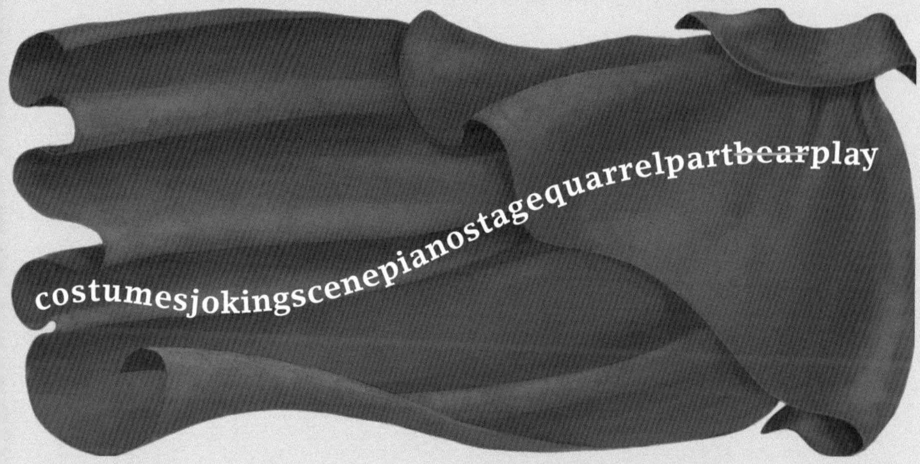

a Maria cannot ....bear.... to think of marrying Mr Rushworth. It's an awful idea for her.

b Some people don't agree and .... with each other all the time.

c Mary Crawford loves music and can play the harp and the .... very well.

d John Yates suggests acting in a .... that is all about lovers' promises.

e Tom likes laughing, ... , and making other people laugh.

f A .... is built in Sir Thomas's library for the actors to stand on.

g Mrs Norris helps to sew the .... for the actors to wear.

h In the end Edmund agrees to take the .... of Mary's lover.

i Poor Fanny has to watch Edmund read aloud his love .... with Mary.

GUESS WHAT

What do you think happens in the next chapter? Tick the boxes.

	Yes	No
a Sir Thomas tells Yates to leave.	☐	☐
b Mrs Norris says she is sorry.	☐	☐
c Maria refuses to marry Mr Rushworth.	☐	☐
d Fanny goes to a dinner party.	☐	☐
e Henry falls in love with Fanny.	☐	☐
f William is invited to Mansfield Park.	☐	☐

Chapter 6
Mr Crawford's plan

Sir Thomas was in the house! It was a moment of **horror** for all in the room. 'What will he say about the play?' was the question they were all thinking.

Henry and Mary Crawford decided this was a good time for them to return to the Parsonage, and left the house, unnoticed. Yates stayed in the library, while everyone else went into the hall to welcome home the head of the family.

Sir Thomas was delighted to be home again. He asked how all his family were. There seemed to be no danger of his finding out about the play just then.

But suddenly he said, 'I'm sorry to leave you all like this, but I really must go and take a look at my library. I missed having my own quiet room in Antigua.' And before they could say a word, he was gone.

Fearing the worst, they all followed. They found him staring in horror at the stage, at the costumes thrown untidily over the chairs, and at Yates, who was loudly rehearsing his part. Tom stepped forward to introduce Yates to his father, who clearly did not think highly of his son's friend. Yates took the opportunity to explain all about the play. He was not intelligent enough to notice that – behind Sir Thomas's back – the others were trying to stop him talking about it. Sir Thomas listened politely, but his face was serious.

He said nothing at the time, but the next day he spoke to Edmund. 'There will be no more acting in this house,' he said. 'The stage must go, and Mrs Norris can give the costumes away.'

'I can only say how sorry I am, sir,' said Edmund unhappily. 'I knew it was wrong, but I was persuaded to agree to it. But *Fanny* has always respected your wishes. Don't be angry with *her*.'

horror a feeling of great fear or shock

Sir Thomas accepted Edmund's **apology** and said no more to any of his children. But he did speak to Mrs Norris about it.

'I am surprised that *you* gave your consent to this play-acting,' he said.

For the first time in her life Mrs Norris did not know what to say. 'Well, you see, Sir Thomas . . . well, er–' Then she thought of a way of changing the **subject**. 'Your daughters wanted to act, so of course I agreed. Ah, how lucky that I made it my business to bring dear Maria and Mr Rushworth together! It was all my doing, you know, Sir Thomas. When I saw his admiration for Maria, I helped things along in every possible way. And now the dear young **couple** are happily engaged! You must thank me for *that*, Sir Thomas!'

'Yes, I am sure we are all very grateful to you, Mrs Norris,' replied the baronet quickly, in order to stop her saying any more about it.

That evening was quieter than usual at Mansfield Park. Maria was worried. She was expecting Henry Crawford to ask her to marry him; in her opinion, he had shown he loved her while they were acting together. Mr Rushworth had gone home to Sotherton, and she hoped he would not need to return. But a whole day had passed, and Henry had stayed away.

At last he arrived, and with delight she saw her father talking to the man she loved. But her happiness did not last long. After speaking to Sir Thomas, Henry told Tom he was going to visit an uncle in Bath. He said goodbye to them all, and was soon gone. So ended all the hopes of Maria and Julia Bertram.

The next day Yates left, and Sir Thomas was pleased to see him go. But the baronet had other worries. By now he had discovered what a very stupid young man Mr Rushworth was, and he wondered how Maria really felt about her fiancé.

'Maria,' he said kindly to her, 'if you no longer wish to marry Mr Rushworth, just tell me.'

apology when you say that you are sorry for something you have done

subject the thing that people are talking about

couple a man and a woman

determined having decided to do something

'Thank you, sir,' replied Maria after only a moment's thought, 'but I have the greatest respect for Mr Rushworth, and every intention of marrying him.' Now that she had no hope of marrying Henry Crawford, she was **determined** to escape from Mansfield Park and her father's influence. Marrying Mr Rushworth seemed to her now the best way of doing that.

Her father accepted her answer as an honest one, and hoped that Mr Rushworth would improve as he got older.

Two months later, Maria Bertram married Mr Rushworth at Sotherton church. The young couple moved to Brighton, a town on the south coast, for several weeks. Julia was invited to join them, because Maria needed a more interesting companion than her husband. The two sisters – enemies when charming Mr Crawford had been around – were close friends once more.

Fanny was now the only young woman at Mansfield Park. The family began to notice her and listen to her opinions far more than before. She was also welcomed warmly as a guest at the Parsonage. Mrs Grant was finding it difficult to keep her sister Mary amused during the long wet autumn, so she often invited Fanny.

One day Mrs Grant happened to invite Edmund to dinner that evening, and then remembered Fanny. 'Would you like to come too, Miss Price?' she asked kindly.

Fanny was surprised and **embarrassed**; no one had invited her to dinner before. But Edmund persuaded Fanny to accept.

He now had to use his influence with his mother, to let Fanny go out that evening.

'But how will I manage without her?' asked Lady Bertram.

'Mrs Norris will be with you, ma'am.'

'I'm surprised that Mrs Grant should ask Fanny at all.'

Sir Thomas did not think it surprising. 'Nothing, in my opinion, could be more natural. Mrs Grant is showing politeness to our niece. Of course Fanny should go.'

Mrs Norris was very cross when she heard of the plan. 'Well, Fanny, you should be very grateful to Mrs Grant for inviting you and to your aunt for letting you go. Make sure you don't talk too much – don't think you're anyone important. And if it rains – it looks like a wet evening to me – don't expect to have the carriage!'

Fanny agreed with everything her aunt said. And when Sir Thomas said to her later, 'Fanny, what time would you like the carriage?' she was very surprised.

'My dear Sir Thomas!' cried Mrs Norris, red with anger. 'Fanny can walk.'

'Walk!?' repeated Sir Thomas. 'I can't expect my niece to walk to a dinner party at this time of year! Will twenty past four suit you, Fanny?'

'Yes, sir,' Fanny whispered.

'Unnecessary! Much too kind!' said Mrs Norris, when Sir Thomas

embarrassed feeling shy or worried about what other people think of you

had left the room. 'But Edmund is going, so it's for him, I suppose.'

But Fanny knew in her heart that the carriage was for *her*, and she felt very grateful to her uncle.

On the way to the Parsonage, Edmund looked kindly at Fanny and admired her dress. 'It's very pretty, Fanny. Hasn't Miss Crawford got one like it?' For a moment Fanny felt sad, but she was pleased at least that Edmund liked her dress.

The evening went well for her. The Grants and their guests enjoyed talking, so she was able to look around her and listen. Henry Crawford had just arrived for another visit. He tried to talk to Fanny about the play, but she was determined not to have a conversation with him. She wanted to hear what Edmund was saying to Dr Grant about the living he would soon take up.

'I'll be ordained in a few weeks,' Edmund was saying.

Just then Fanny noticed Mary Crawford's face. It had lost all its colour. 'She hates the idea of him becoming a clergyman!' thought Fanny. 'He and she could never be happy together.'

The evening ended with a pleasant drive home in the carriage, and Fanny had much to think about as she went to bed.

The next morning Henry Crawford said to his sister, 'I've decided to stay here a few weeks longer, Mary.'

'Ah, to walk and ride with me, I hope?'

'I'll be happy to do that. But I have a more important plan. I want to make Fanny Price fall in love with me.'

'Fanny Price! Really, Henry! You ought to be **satisfied** with her two cousins.'

'But I can't be satisfied without her. You haven't realized how much she's improved in the last six weeks – she's beautiful now. But even if I do my best to flatter her, she doesn't smile at me. She's so different from all the other girls I've met! I'm determined to make a small hole in her heart.'

'Well, don't make her really unhappy, Henry. She's a sweet girl, and a dear friend of mine.'

In the next few days Henry tried very hard to make Fanny like him. And although Fanny had not forgotten his bad behaviour in the past, she was ready to be polite to him.

But she had someone else to think of – her brother William, who was now in the navy. His ship had returned to England, and Sir Thomas had invited him to stay at Mansfield Park. Soon her dear brother was actually there with her. Fanny cried when she first saw him, and spent most of her time at his side.

Sir Thomas was pleased with William, who was a fine-looking, honest, respectful young man. All the family listened in admiration as William described the dangers of life at sea. Henry Crawford watched Fanny, and saw that her lovely eyes never left her brother's

satisfied happy because you did something that you wanted

face. 'What a girl!' he thought. 'If I can only make her fall in love with me!' He tried harder than ever to please Fanny. Even Sir Thomas, who was usually too grand to notice these things, began to think that Mr Crawford was interested in his niece.

One day Sir Thomas was listening to a conversation between Fanny and William.

'I don't know if I'll ever get a **commission**, Fanny,' William was saying sadly. 'But I must become an officer if I'm to have a real future in the navy!'

'Oh my dear William, don't be sad. I'm sure our uncle will help you get a commission if he can.'

'Do you like dancing, Fanny?'

'Yes, very much. But I get tired quickly.'

'I'd like to see you dance. Don't you ever have any balls round here?' Then he noticed Sir Thomas was nearby, and asked him, 'Is Fanny a very good dancer, sir?'

Fanny was very embarrassed. But her uncle said calmly, 'I'm afraid I haven't seen Fanny dance since she was a child.'

'*I* have had the **pleasure** of seeing your sister dance, Mr Price,' said Henry Crawford, who was also listening. 'But I can't tell you about it in front of everyone, because I know she doesn't like people talking about her.'

In fact Henry Crawford had only seen Fanny at a ball once and he could not really remember very clearly how Fanny had danced there. But his polite and charming words made Sir Thomas feel sure he admired Fanny, and that gave the baronet an idea.

The next day he told his family that he was giving a ball at Mansfield Park, for Fanny and William. Fanny thought it was almost too great an **honour**. 'My first ball!' she thought. 'I'll dance with William, and Edmund, I hope. But I'll have to talk to so many important people, and everyone will look at me! And what shall I wear?'

commission
a paper that makes a soldier or sailor into an officer

pleasure
happiness

honour
something that makes you feel special and pleased

But when the day of the ball arrived, Fanny really began to enjoy herself. She wore a new dress. And round her neck she wore a **cross** which William had given her, on a **chain** which Edmund had given her – presents from the two people who were dearest in the world to her. Another chain which Mary Crawford had given Fanny to wear – an old present from Henry – lay upstairs in Fanny's room, still in its box.

cross a shape where two lines meet, like this †; Christians sometimes wear one on a chain around the neck

chain a long string of metal rings which are joined together

The ball went much better than she had expected. She had to dance with Henry Crawford. But he spoke politely and gently to her, and she realized how much his behaviour had improved. Sir Thomas felt very **proud** of his niece, and he was sure that Mr Crawford was in love with her. 'It's just a question of time before he asks to marry her,' he thought.

proud happy about something that someone has done

ACTIVITIES

READING CHECK

Circle the best words to complete these sentences.

a Sir Thomas listens politely to *Henry / Yates / Tom* explaining about the play.

b Mrs Norris is proud of introducing *Maria and Mr Rushworth / Edmund and Mary / Julia and John Yates* to each other.

c Maria is determined to *live abroad / escape from her family / make some new friends in London.*

d Edmund wants Fanny to *accept Mrs Grant's invitation / stay at home with Lady Bertram / be more polite to Mrs Norris.*

e Sir Thomas orders the carriage for *Edmund / Mrs Norris / Fanny.*

f Henry tells his sister about his plan to make Fanny *talk about him to Maria / hate him / fall in love with him.*

g William tells the Bertram family about his *adventures at sea / life in Portsmouth / problems with money.*

h Sir Thomas gives *a ball for / some of his fortune to / a valuable present to* Fanny and William.

i At the ball Fanny wears a chain that *Edmund has given her / she has bought for herself / Mary has lent her.*

WORD WORK

1 Use the words around the carriage to complete the sentences.

a You make an ..apology.. when you want to tell someone that you feel sorry about something.

b You may feel .... if a lot of people look at you and you aren't used to that.

c When you are happy, you are full of a feeling of ....

d Sometimes we change the .... of the conversation when we don't want to talk about something.

e Parents are usually .... of their children when they do something well.

f Some people are very .... ! They decide that they will do something, and then they do it.

g It is an .... to be invited to a friend's wedding. Usually only special friends and family are asked.

Use the pictures to complete the puzzle.

Across

5

4
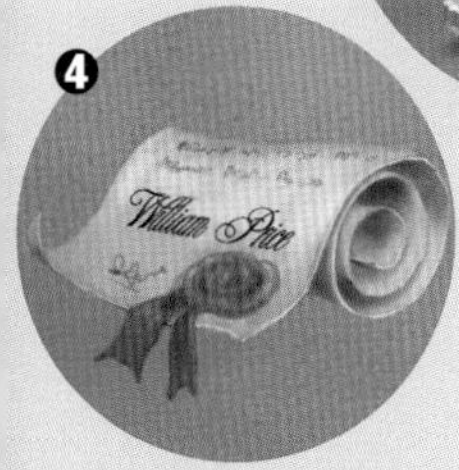

Down

1
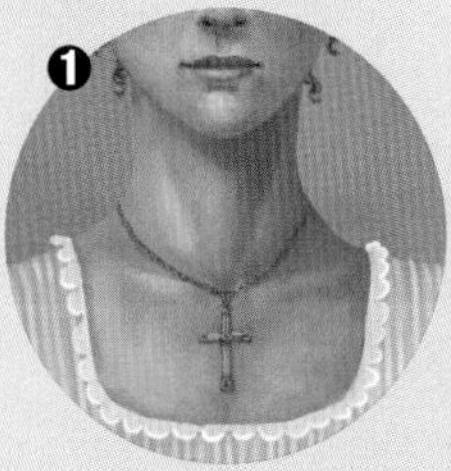

2
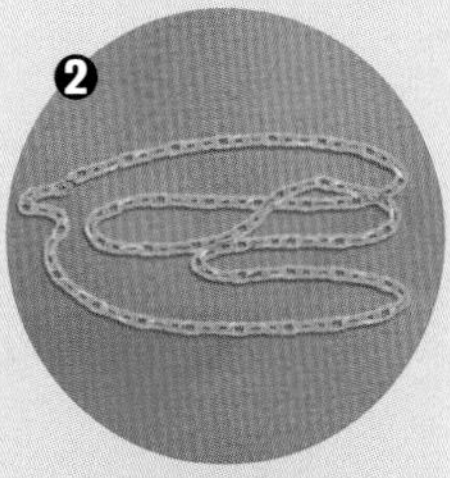

3
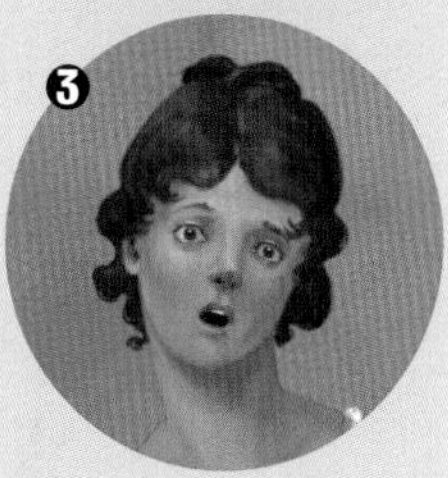

GUESS WHAT

What do you think happens in the next chapter? Tick two boxes.

- **a** Sir Thomas gets a commission for William. ☐
- **b** Henry asks Fanny to marry him. ☐
- **c** Mary becomes more hopeful that Edmund loves her. ☐
- **d** William tries to persuade Fanny to accept the offer of marriage. ☐
- **e** Mary shows her feelings about Edmund to Lady Bertram. ☐

Chapter 7
A proposal of marriage

The day after the ball Henry Crawford went to London on business, William returned to his ship, and Edmund went to stay with a friend, Mr Owen, for a few days. Mary Crawford found she missed Edmund very much. When a week passed with no news of his return, she decided to ask Fanny about him.

'Are you surprised that your cousin is staying so long at Mr Owen's?' she said, as lightly as she could.

'Not really,' replied Fanny.

'But Mr Owen has three daughters, I hear. I expect they are all very pretty. Perhaps they sing well, and play the piano, the harp, or some other instrument.'

'I know nothing of the Miss Owens,' replied Fanny calmly.

'I shall have to leave Mansfield soon myself. I'm sorry I won't see your cousin again before I leave.'

Fanny's honesty made her say, 'You know that people here will miss you greatly.'

Miss Crawford waited for more. But when Fanny was silent, she said with a laugh, 'Oh well, anyone who wants to see me will be able to find me!' There was another short silence. 'I don't wonder at the Miss Owens. A baronet's younger son is somebody important, even if he is a clergyman. What do you think, Miss Price? Do you think your cousin Edmund will marry soon?'

'No, I don't,' said Fanny softly, hoping she was right.

Her companion looked happier at this, and changed the subject.

That evening Mary's brother returned from London. The first thing he did was to visit Mansfield Park.

'Why were you there so long?' Mary asked him crossly, when he finally arrived at the Parsonage.

'I didn't want to leave any earlier – Fanny looked so lovely! I must tell you, Mary – I am determined to marry Fanny Price.'

Mary's surprise soon changed to pleasure. 'Lucky, lucky girl!' she cried. 'And you will have the sweetest little wife, who will be very grateful to you! Does she know yet?'

'No.'

'What are you waiting for? Take the first opportunity to **propose** to her, Henry. She will never have the heart to refuse.'

'I will, Mary.'

The next morning Henry was at Mansfield Park again, much earlier than the usual visiting hour. Luckily for him, he found Fanny alone.

propose to ask someone to marry you

'My dear Miss Price,' he said, 'it is with great delight that I bring you this news. I have here a commission for your brother William. Would you like to see it?'

Fanny could not speak, but took the papers with a shaking hand. While she read them, Crawford said, 'This was my reason for going to London.'

'So *you* have done this!' cried Fanny. 'How very, very kind! How did you manage it?'

'My uncle is an **admiral**, you know – Admiral Crawford – and I told him about your brother. He agreed that William would make a fine officer. So he spoke to all the right people, and the **result** is this commission!' He took Fanny's hand. 'I wanted to help your brother, Miss Price, but I had another reason for doing it. I'm sure you can guess it.'

At first Fanny did not understand what he meant. But soon it became all too clear.

'Everything I've done has been for you, Miss Price! I've never felt a love as strong as this before! Say that you like me, say that you love me! I offer myself, my hand, my heart, my **fortune** to you!'

admiral a very important officer in the navy

result what happens because of something that you do

fortune money, houses, and valuable things that make you a rich person

Fanny did not think he was serious. 'No, no, no,' she cried, hiding her face. 'Don't say any more! I know it's all untrue. You're only flattering me. You don't really feel for me in that way.'

She pulled away from him and ran out of the room. She felt very **confused**, and hoped Mr Crawford would never speak to her again like that. 'He's probably talked of love like that to fifty other women!' she told herself. But there was one thing at least she *could* be happy about in all of this – William was going to be an officer at last.

confused not thinking clearly

The next morning Fanny woke early. 'I hope Mr Crawford and his sister will leave Mansfield soon,' she thought. 'Then my worries will be at an end.' But when she looked out of her sitting room window, she saw Mr Crawford coming to the house. 'Why has he come so early?' she wondered. She was determined to stay in her room, and not to talk to him.

After half an hour or so, there was a heavy step outside her sitting room, and her uncle entered.

'My dear Fanny, Mr Crawford has visited me this morning. I have pleasure in telling you, he greatly admires you and proposes to marry you. I must say, he's an excellent young man, with a very fine fortune. He's in the library, and is hoping to see you there.'

'Oh no, sir, I cannot see him!' cried Fanny wildly. 'Mr Crawford knows – I told him yesterday – I don't want to hear his proposal!'

Sir Thomas was very surprised. 'Do you mean, Fanny, that you're going to *refuse* Mr Crawford?'

'Yes, sir.'

'For what reason, may I ask?'

'I – I do not like him enough to marry him, sir.'

'This is very strange,' replied Sir Thomas coldly. 'Here is a young man who is well known to us, who is liked by everybody, and who moves in the best social circles. I cannot understand why *you* do not like him.'

character a person's special qualities

disappointed sad because someone or something is worse than you expected

sob to cry sadly, loudly and suddenly; a loud, sad, sudden cry

Fanny said nothing. 'I can't explain about Mr Crawford's true **character**,' she thought, 'because it means telling him about Maria's and Julia's bad behaviour!'

'Up to now I've had a very good opinion of you, Fanny,' her uncle went on. 'I thought you were a good, respectful girl. But now I'm **disappointed** in you. You're thinking only of yourself. What about your family? They want you to make a good marriage, and to help them if you can. You seem ungrateful to me. All these years Lady Bertram and I have taken care of you. It is your duty to respect our wishes. You will never have a better proposal than this, and I think you should accept it.'

But Fanny **sobbed** and sobbed, saying she could never accept Mr Crawford. Sir Thomas began to feel sorry for her, when he saw how miserable she was. He went downstairs to the library to tell Mr Crawford that Fanny was not ready to accept his proposal yet.

In the next few days Fanny had much to bear. Mr Crawford repeated his proposal to her. And although she explained to him that they could never be happy together, he was still determined to persuade her in time. Sir Thomas told Fanny there was no question of making her marry against her wishes; she must decide for herself.

Many surprises were waiting for Edmund when he returned home. The first was seeing Miss Crawford. He had expected her to be in London by now. She welcomed him with delight, and this made him feel more hopeful again.

He was also very pleased to hear of William's commission, which all the family were talking about.

But the greatest surprise was Henry Crawford's proposal of marriage. Sir Thomas asked Edmund to use his influence with Fanny to persuade her to accept.

'Dear Fanny,' Edmund said to her later the next day, 'I know you're worried about Crawford's proposal. I think it's a very honest one. But of course you should refuse him if you really can't love him.'

'Oh Edmund! I'm so happy to hear you say that! I thought you were against me, like your father.'

'No, Fanny. But think of this – Crawford really loves you and wants to make you happy. Let him succeed, Fanny!'

'Oh, never! He will never persuade me! We are so very different!'

'Well, I think it may sometimes be good to have a husband and wife who see things differently.'

Fanny knew he was thinking of himself and Mary Crawford. 'I must say, cousin,' she said, 'that I don't like his character. I haven't thought well of him since the play. He made both Maria and Julia think he was in love with them!'

'Don't think of that time, Fanny, we were all doing wrong then. Think of Crawford's warm heart! He will make you a happy woman, Fanny, but you – you will make him a good man! It's what his sister wants too. She speaks so lovingly of you, Fanny!'

Fanny was too tired and miserable to reply. She could not bear to hear Edmund speak admiringly of Miss Crawford. 'Perhaps he'll propose to her before she leaves Mansfield,' she thought sadly.

ACTIVITIES

READING CHECK

Correct the mistakes in these sentences.

a Mary Crawford misses ~~her brother~~ Edmund very much while he is away.

b Mary thinks that Fanny will refuse Henry's offer of marriage.

c Henry's father is an important officer in the navy.

d Fanny thinks that Henry has talked of love to no other women.

e Sir Thomas feels that Henry is an unsuitable husband for Fanny.

f Edmund agrees with Fanny that money is necessary in a marriage.

g Fanny is sure that she could be happy with Henry.

h Fanny thinks that Edmund will forget Mary one day.

WORD WORK

Use the words around the window to complete Fanny's diary.

Oh, I'm so unhappy! Why did Mr Crawford **a)** propose *to me? Why does he want to marry me? I don't think he really loves me. And I can't marry a man with a bad* **b)** .... *that people talk about, even if he has a large* **c)** .... *Money isn't everything after all! But it was very kind of him to go and ask his uncle the* **d)** .... *to help dear William in the Navy. And the* **e)** .... *of his help is that William is going to be an officer! I don't know what to do! I'm so* **f)** .... *I'm afraid Sir Thomas is* **g)** .... *with me. He thought that I would do better than this. Oh dear, I'm crying now. I must try not to* **h)** .... *so loudly!*

GUESS WHAT

What do you think happens in the next chapter? Tick the boxes.

a Fanny ...
- **1** decides to accept Henry's proposal. ☐
- **2** gives Mary a message from Edmund. ☐
- **3** goes to visit her family in Portsmouth. ☐

b Edmund ...
- **1** proposes to Mary. ☐
- **2** writes a letter to Fanny. ☐
- **3** meets Fanny's sister, Susan. ☐

c Mary ...
- **1** often sees Edmund in London. ☐
- **2** gets angry with Fanny. ☐
- **3** discovers Fanny's secret. ☐

d Tom ...
- **1** falls in love. ☐
- **2** loses money at the races. ☐
- **3** has a riding accident. ☐

Chapter 8
A family visit

The day after Edmund returned to Mansfield, Mary Crawford came to visit Fanny in her small sitting room upstairs. Fanny was afraid that Mary would be angry with her for refusing her brother Henry's proposal of marriage. But instead of talking about that, Mary looked around her, dreamily.

'It was here in this room that we rehearsed our love scene, your cousin Edmund and I,' she said softly. 'I shall never forget those happy moments! Oh, why must such times pass!'

Fanny's face coloured as she too remembered.

Then Mary shook herself and said with a smile, 'I feel sure that you and I will be sisters, Fanny. You're closer to me than all my fashionable London friends. Good, gentle Fanny! I hate to leave you.'

Fanny felt the influence of these loving words, and gave a small sob.

'Don't cry, Fanny! Oh, I wish you could see how angry half the young women in London are, now that Henry's in love with you! Soon you'll decide you love him, won't you, Fanny? He loves you with all his heart. And remember, he got your brother's commission.'

'Oh yes! I am most grateful to him for that!' said Fanny feelingly.

'Well, I must leave you now, dear Fanny. Write to me in London. I expect I'll see your cousin Edmund there.'

It was over, and Mary had not guessed Fanny's love for Edmund. The Crawfords left Mansfield the following morning.

On the same day, Fanny's brother William arrived for a ten-day holiday, so she was able to forget about Mr Crawford for a while. But Sir Thomas did not want her to forget him. He had a plan which, he hoped, would persuade her to think more kindly of Mr Crawford's proposal. He suggested that, when William returned to his ship in Portsmouth, Fanny should travel with him and spend

some time with her family there. 'She has lived in a very comfortable home for the last few years,' he thought. 'Perhaps she'll have a better opinion of Mr Crawford and his income after staying with her family and seeing how poor people live.'

Fanny agreed to the plan with delight, and looked forward to

control to make people do what you want, or to make things happen as you want

swear (*past* **swore**) to use bad language

alcohol strong drink, like beer, or wine

get used to to find something not unusual any more

seeing her dear family again. Everyone liked the idea, except Lady Bertram. 'I don't know how I'll manage without Fanny!' she said.

'But *I* can be your companion, my dear sister,' offered Mrs Norris. And so it was decided.

In a few days' time, Fanny and William were on their way. The journey took two days, and by the time they arrived at the Prices' small house in Portsmouth, they were both very tired.

Fanny's mother welcomed her warmly, but her younger brothers and sisters did not remember her well. She was left in a dark corner of the sitting room, while the boys ran around shouting and the girls argued among themselves. Mrs Price and her servant were busy packing the clothes that William was taking back to his ship. Mr Price spoke a few words to Fanny, but soon returned to reading his newspaper.

Fanny felt disappointed and miserable. No one seemed interested in her. What a home it was: an untidy little house in a back street, full of noisy, quarrelling children, with a dirty-looking servant who did not obey orders! Her mother could not **control** her large family, and looked tired. Her father often **swore** in a loud voice, and smelt of **alcohol**.

Fanny thought sadly of Mansfield Park – her kind uncle and aunt, the beautiful rooms, the well-cooked meals, the polite servants, the intelligent conversation. 'I miss it all so much!' she said to herself.

But as the days went by, she began to **get used to** her new life. She spent much of her time with her fourteen-year-old sister, Susan. This young girl had realized how much was wrong at home, and was trying to put things right. Fanny found she had a good influence on Susan, and under her care, her young sister improved greatly. Together they read books, did their sewing, and talked about all kinds of things. Time passed, and Fanny tried not to think about Mr Crawford's proposal.

Seven weeks after her arrival in Portsmouth, a letter from Edmund arrived.

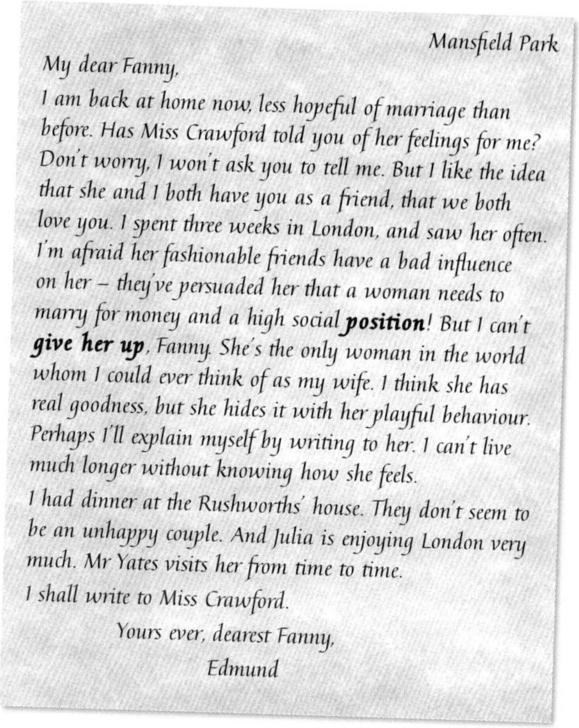

Mansfield Park

My dear Fanny,

I am back at home now, less hopeful of marriage than before. Has Miss Crawford told you of her feelings for me? Don't worry, I won't ask you to tell me. But I like the idea that she and I both have you as a friend, that we both love you. I spent three weeks in London, and saw her often. I'm afraid her fashionable friends have a bad influence on her – they've persuaded her that a woman needs to marry for money and a high social ***position****! But I can't* ***give her up****, Fanny. She's the only woman in the world whom I could ever think of as my wife. I think she has real goodness, but she hides it with her playful behaviour. Perhaps I'll explain myself by writing to her. I can't live much longer without knowing how she feels.*

I had dinner at the Rushworths' house. They don't seem to be an unhappy couple. And Julia is enjoying London very much. Mr Yates visits her from time to time.

I shall write to Miss Crawford.

Yours ever, dearest Fanny,

Edmund

Fanny could not control herself. She sobbed bitterly as she read his letter. 'He can't give her up! Oh, he'll marry her, and be poor and miserable all his life! The only woman in the world he could ever think of as his wife! Oh, Edmund!'

More bad news arrived a few days later, in a letter from Lady Bertram. She told Fanny that Tom Bertram had fallen from his horse while on

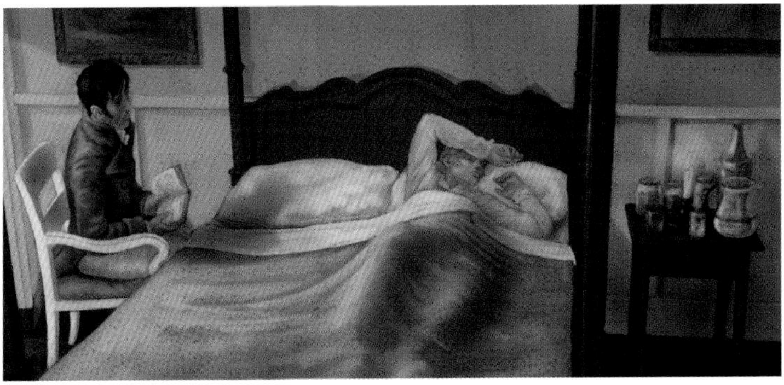

a visit to the races. After a lot of drinking, two friends had carried him to another friend's house, and had left him there, with only servants to take care of him. He had caught a **fever**, and was now seriously ill. Sir Thomas had gone in a carriage to fetch him, and Tom was now safely back at Mansfield Park. But the doctors said that his life was in great danger.

position the place that someone or something is in

give someone up to accept that you cannot marry someone

fever when you get very hot because you are ill

READING CHECK

Choose the best answer to complete the sentences.

a Mary hopes that Fanny …
- **1** will visit her in London. ☐
- **2** will agree to marry Henry. ☑
- **3** will persuade Edmund to propose to her. ☐

b Sir Thomas's plan is to show Fanny …
- **1** how much her family loves her. ☐
- **2** how useful Henry's fortune will be. ☐
- **3** how easy it is to travel. ☐

c Fanny doesn't enjoy her stay in Portsmouth because …
- **1** she misses Mansfield Park. ☐
- **2** she has nobody to talk to. ☐
- **3** she has to do all the housework. ☐

d Edmund thinks that Mary …
- **1** is a good friend of Fanny's. ☐
- **2** will be the perfect wife for him. ☐
- **3** is never influenced by her friends. ☐

e When Fanny gets Edmund's letter, she's unhappy because …
- **1** he hasn't written before. ☐
- **2** she feels sorry for Maria. ☐
- **3** she's afraid that Edmund loves Mary. ☐

f The Bertrams are worried about Tom because …
- **1** he's very ill. ☐
- **2** he's away from home. ☐
- **3** he's spending too much money. ☐

ACTIVITIES

WORD WORK

Find words in the square to complete the sentences.

A	C	F	G	J	O	N	D	I
P	O	S	I	T	I	O	N	X
C	N	D	V	B	T	H	E	A
G	T	F	E	V	E	R	M	L
Q	R	S	O	V	H	U	Z	C
W	O	C	N	A	S	B	Y	O
E	L	F	E	J	W	O	U	H
G	E	T	U	S	E	D	T	O
A	W	C	P	Q	A	M	L	L
K	N	X	E	O	R	I	K	H

a Small children can be hard to ..control.. . They do what they want to do.

b If you move to a different country, you soon .... it, and it doesn't seem strange any more.

c My cousin holds an important .... in his company. It's an interesting job and he's paid well for it too.

d Our son's ill with a .... Feel his head. It's so hot!

e You can't marry *two* men – you'll have to .... !

f You shouldn't drive after drinking .... You can't think clearly. It's very dangerous.

g It's always rude to .... at people. Using bad language is never a good idea.

GUESS WHAT

Make four sentences with these phrases and find out what happens in the next chapter.

a Tom
b Mary
c Fanny
d Henry

1 visits Maria
2 wants to go
3 is very ill
4 warns Fanny

i not to listen to what some people say.
ii while her husband is away.
iii and help the Bertram family.
iv but slowly gets better.

Chapter 9
News from London

About a week after she heard about Tom's fall and illness, Fanny **received** a second letter from Edmund. He told her that Tom's fever had gone, but that he was still very seriously ill. Edmund was spending most of his time by Tom's bedside, and when she read these words, Fanny loved Edmund all the more for his care of his brother. She noticed sadly that, even in these difficult times, Mary was not far from Edmund's thoughts. At the end of the letter, Edmund had written:

'In my last letter I wrote to you about my feelings for Miss Crawford. Well, I started to write to her, but I fear the influence of her friends. If she asks them what she should do, they'll persuade her against me. So I've decided that, when Tom is better, I'll go to London and speak to her there myself.'

The weeks passed, and Tom's health improved painfully slowly. Fanny hoped that when **Easter** came, her uncle would send a carriage to fetch her. It would soon be almost three months that she had been away from Mansfield Park. She knew how useful she could be there – playing cards with Lady Bertram to amuse her, reading to poor, sick Tom, listening to Mrs Norris, taking messages from one end of the house to another. She **longed** to be there, with all the family. Now she realized that Portsmouth was just Portsmouth, but Mansfield Park was home.

But Easter was very late this year, and there was still no word from her uncle. 'I suppose he's too worried about Tom to think of me,' she thought miserably. 'But what about Tom's sisters? *They* don't seem worried at all! It's easy for *them* to travel, but they both prefer to stay in London!'

receive to get something that somebody sends to you

Easter a spring holiday in the Christian church

long to want something very much

Then, a few days later, Fanny received a letter from Mary Crawford. It said:

London

My dear Fanny,

I write to ask you how things are at Mansfield Park. Of course, this is a worrying time for Tom Bertram's family. People here are saying that he's in danger of dying. Is that true? I need not say how pleased I shall be if there has been any mistake. Now don't smile like that, Fanny, I promise you I've never **bribed** *a doctor in my life! It's always sad when a young man dies. But I can't help thinking that 'Sir Edmund' would do more good with the Bertram fortune than his older brother 'Sir Tom'. Write to me by return of post with your answer – I need to know as soon as possible.*

Henry tells me he's visited Maria Rushworth, who's spending the Easter holiday with some friends – her husband is away at the moment. Now don't be **jealous** *– Henry loves only you, and he's wild to see you again. Dear Fanny, if you want to return to Mansfield Park, just let me know. Henry and I can take you there in his carriage, and stay a few days at the Parsonage. It will be no trouble, and we can see our friends at Mansfield Park. I think Edmund would be in London, if Tom weren't ill – don't you agree?*

Yours ever,

Mary

Fanny was **disgusted** by this letter. It showed the true characters of both Henry and Mary Crawford in the clearest possible light. Mary had a cold-hearted interest in money and social position. She was suddenly eager to marry Edmund, if he became a baronet and had a large fortune. 'Bribing a doctor!' thought Fanny in horror. 'How can she joke about that kind of thing, and talk so lightly of Tom's death!' And Henry was continuing his bad behaviour with Maria, now a married woman. Far from feeling jealous, Fanny was disappointed in him; she had thought his character was improving.

bribe to pay money to someone secretly to make them do something for you

jealous feeling angry or unhappy because someone you like is interested in someone else

disgusted made angry or sick by something that you really do not like

There was no difficulty about her reply. She wrote a few short lines, describing honestly the seriousness of Tom's illness, and politely refusing Miss Crawford's offer to take her back to Mansfield. She knew she must wait for her uncle to decide when she should return.

Fanny thought Miss Crawford would write again, to ask for more information and to repeat her offer. Sure enough, a week later she received a second letter from Mary. As she opened it, she was surprised to see how short it was. This was the letter:

London

Dear Fanny,

A most unpleasant **rumour** *has reached me, and I'm writing now to warn you not to listen to it if it reaches you. I expect there is some mistake, and in a day or two it will all be clear. I'm sure Henry has done nothing wrong – maybe his head was turned for a moment, but I know he thinks of no one except you. Don't say a word to anyone about this, don't even whisper it, until I write again. It will all quieten down and the only thing that people will remember about it all is that Mr Rushworth was so stupid! Perhaps they've gone to Mansfield Park, and perhaps Julia is with them. But why didn't you let us fetch you from Portsmouth? I hope you aren't going to* **regret** *it.*

Yours ever,

Mary

Fanny looked up from her reading in horror. No unpleasant rumour had reached *her*, so she did not fully understand this strange letter. She could only guess that something very bad had happened. 'What could it be?' she wondered. 'Is it the Rushworths who've gone away? And what has Mr Crawford done? Oh dear, this rumour will worry them all at Mansfield Park! I really hope Mary writes again soon. I must know what's happened!'

rumour a story that may not be true, but that people like to tell

regret to be sorry that something happened, or to feel sorry about something

ACTIVITIES

READING CHECK

1 Match the first and second parts of these sentences.

a Edmund decides to …	**1** worried about Tom's illness.
b Fanny wants to …	**2** find out Mary's feelings for him.
c Maria and Julia don't seem …	**3** keep away from Maria.
d Mary wants Edmund to …	**4** go home to help the Bertrams.
e Mary offers to …	**5** give her more facts.
f Henry can't seem to …	**6** take Fanny back to Mansfield Park.
g Mary is afraid that …	**7** become a baronet instead of Tom.
h Fanny wants Mary to …	**8** something bad has happened.

2 Are these sentences true or false? Tick the boxes.

	True	**False**
a Tom is in good health now.	☐	☑
b Fanny is delighted with Mary's first letter.	☐	☐
c Fanny understands her uncle's feelings.	☐	☐
d Mary will be pleased if Tom dies.	☐	☐
e Fanny is very worried about the Bertrams.	☐	☐

WORD WORK

Find words in the puzzle to complete the sentences on page 63.

gu	ous	re	bing	ret
ur	ves	ru	ster	dis
cei	lo	bri	reg	ngs
ed	st	Ea	mo	jeal

a Fanny receives several letters from different people while she is in Portsmouth.

b Fanny is looking forward to seeing Mansfield Park again in the spring – at .... time.

c Fanny .... to be back with the Bertrams. She can't wait to leave Portsmouth.

d Mary Crawford jokes about .... a doctor with some money to kill Tom.

e Mary thinks Fanny may be .... of Henry's interest in Maria, but Fanny is not worried or angry about that.

f Fanny feels sick because she is .... by Mary's letter, which shows her true and unpleasant character.

g Mary writes about a .... that she has heard some people talking about.

h Fanny does not .... refusing Henry's proposal. She feels good about what she did.

GUESS WHAT

What do you think happens in the next chapter? Tick four sentences.

a Maria marries Henry. ☐

b Julia runs away with John Yates. ☐

c Tom gets ill again and dies. ☐

d Mr Rushworth divorces Maria. ☐

e Mary persuades Edmund to marry her. ☐

f Fanny marries the man she loves. ☐

g Susan becomes Lady Bertram's companion. ☐

Chapter 10
Two more weddings

The next day came, but there was no letter for Fanny, either from Mary Crawford or from Mansfield Park. Fanny was very disappointed; she could think of nothing but that strange and terrible rumour that Mary had talked about. What could it be? In the afternoon her father brought the daily newspaper home. Fanny sat in the hot, dirty sitting room, with a headache, while he read it.

Suddenly he said, 'What's the name of your rich cousins in London, Fanny?'

'Rushworth, sir.'

'Well, they're very fine people, to be sure! It says here that Mrs Rushworth has left her husband's house. It seems she's run away with a Mr Crawford! What will the great Sir Thomas think of *that?*'

'There must be some mistake!' cried Fanny. But when she read the report herself, she knew it was true. She was too **shocked** and disgusted to say any more. *Now* she understood Miss Crawford's letter clearly. *Now* she could see her own earlier mistake about who had gone away – it was not Mr and Mrs Rushworth, it was Mrs Rushworth and Henry Crawford.

She did not sleep that night. 'Maria, married for only six months, and Henry, who said he loved me – it's terrible!' she thought feverishly. 'The Bertrams will be so miserable! Sir Thomas will feel the **disgrace** very strongly. And Edmund, poor Edmund . . .' She could not bear to think of *his* feelings.

There was no more news for two days, but on the third day she received a letter from Edmund.

shocked very surprised by something bad

disgrace when other people cannot respect or accept you, because you have done something bad

Mansfield Park

Dear Fanny,

I expect you have heard by now about Maria and Mr Crawford, but I have more bad news to tell you. Julia has ***eloped*** *with Mr Yates! My father wishes you to return home, to be a* ***comfort*** *to my mother at this difficult time. He invites your sister Susan to come with you. I'll be in Portsmouth the morning after you receive this, to bring you both to Mansfield Park. Don't ask me to describe my feelings.*

Yours ever,

Edmund

Fanny was surprised and shocked to hear about Julia. But the good news was that she would see Edmund the next day, and return to her dear Mansfield Park. She now had a lot to do – telling Susan and her parents about the invitation, packing clothes for both of them, and getting everything ready for the journey. She was almost able to forget, for a while, the horror of what Maria Rushworth and Henry Crawford had done.

elope to run away secretly to get married

comfort a person who makes you feel happier when you are sad or worried

Edmund arrived early the next morning. For a moment he held Fanny in his arms, saying, 'Dearest Fanny – my only sister – my only comfort now!' She noticed sadly how ill and unhappy he looked.

Soon all three of them were on their way. With Susan in the carriage, there was no opportunity to talk about Maria, Julia, or the Crawfords. It was a silent journey. Edmund kept his eyes closed most of the time. Fanny looked eagerly out of the window at the road which was bringing her closer to Mansfield Park. Susan was looking forward excitedly to her first visit to the great house.

When they arrived at Mansfield Park, it was clear how miserable everyone there was. Mrs Norris was really the unhappiest of them all. Maria was her favourite, and the marriage to Mr Rushworth was the result of her work. So this disgrace was almost too much for her to bear.

Unusually for her, Lady Bertram was also miserable. But she received Fanny back into the family with delight, and welcomed Susan very kindly. Fanny was able to be a great comfort to her aunt again. Once they had fully discussed the terrible business, Fanny helped her aunt to think of other subjects of conversation. Soon Lady Bertram became calmer.

Fanny also saw how unhappy her poor uncle was. He had been to London to try to find Maria, but with no success. Mr Rushworth was very angry, and wanted a **divorce**. He was determined that Maria should never enter his house again. Sir Thomas had other worries, too. Julia's disgrace was less than Maria's, but in his opinion she had chosen a useless young man to elope with. 'What will happen if Yates refuses to marry her?' he thought.

Then there was Tom, who had been shocked by Maria's behaviour and whose illness had recently got worse. And finally, Sir Thomas was worried about Edmund. He knew his younger son was in love with Miss Crawford, and had no chance of happiness with her now.

Fanny herself was worried about Edmund, too. 'Is he still in love with Miss Crawford?' she wondered. It was fully two days before he began to talk to her on the subject.

'If you don't mind, my dear Fanny, I want to tell you what happened at my last meeting with her,' he said. 'It will be a great **relief** to talk about it. When I went to London with my father to find Maria, Miss Crawford asked me to visit her, so I did. I thought she'd be ashamed of her brother's behaviour, but, oh Fanny, she

divorce when a marriage ends and the husband and wife go different ways

relief when you feel happy that something isn't a problem any more

wasn't! She spoke of it lightly, she even joked about it! She called Henry and Maria stupid, that's all, and wished you'd agreed to marry him. Fanny, I know I was confused before, but my eyes have been opened. I see now what kind of character she has.'

'What happened next?' asked Fanny. She longed to know how the conversation had ended.

'She went on to say that Henry must give you up, of course. She hoped to persuade him to marry Maria!' Edmund stopped, and it was some time before he could speak again. 'In my reply I told her we would never want Maria to marry a man like Henry Crawford. I told her how much she'd hurt me. I hadn't realized how different her opinions were from mine. She has no understanding of honour, and no idea of the disgrace to our family! I said that perhaps it was all for the best – I had less to regret in giving her up. I must say, she looked surprised, and a little embarrassed at that. She said goodbye to me in a laughing, careless way, and I left the room. Just then I heard her voice behind me. "Mr Bertram," she said. I looked round and saw her playful smile, inviting me back. I walked on. I have since – but only for a moment – regretted that I didn't go back. But I know I was right! Thank you for listening, Fanny. This has been the greatest relief to me.'

From now on, Fanny was happy to be at home again, happy to be useful, happy to be safe from Henry Crawford. She was happier still that Edmund now understood Mary Crawford's true character.

Sir Thomas knew he had made mistakes as a father. He had never taught his daughters to think of others, or to do always what was right. The result was that they did not seem to know their duty to the church, their family, or their social position. But there was some good news of Julia. She and Mr Yates were actually married, and she was really sorry for her behaviour. Sir Thomas accepted her apology, and once he'd got used to the idea, he decided that Mr Yates wasn't a bad husband for his younger daughter after all.

He was also happier about Tom, who was now in good health again. Tom's character had improved since his illness and Maria's disgrace. He no longer thought only of himself, and had become a real help to his father.

But there was no easy answer to the problem of Maria. Mr Rushworth got his divorce, but Mr Crawford did not in the end want to marry her. Sir Thomas refused to have her back under his roof. So he decided to buy a small house for her in the country, far from Mansfield, and Mrs Norris went to live with her there. The baronet thought the two women would punish each other more than enough.

Very soon Edmund stopped regretting Mary Crawford, and started thinking about a very different kind of woman. He realized there was someone, who was already very dear to him, who would make a far better wife for him than Miss Crawford. He had no difficulty in persuading Fanny to accept his proposal. She had loved him since she was ten, and her wedding day was the happiest time of her life.

Sir Thomas was highly satisfied with the wife his son had chosen. 'Taking Fanny into my home to bring her up all those years ago was the best thing I ever did!' he told himself proudly. 'She's a better daughter to me than my own girls!'

Even Lady Bertram was persuaded to manage without Fanny, because she now had young Susan to fetch and carry for her.

When Dr Grant died, Edmund was able to take the living at Mansfield. He and Fanny moved into the Parsonage, close to Mansfield Park. With true love, and a good income, and many friends, the young couple were as happy as any young couple could be.

ACTIVITIES

READING CHECK

Match the sentences with the people in the pictures.

Sir Thomas

Mrs Norris

Fanny

Mr Rushworth

Mary Crawford

John Yates

Henry Crawford

Susan

Mr Price

a Mr Price reads in his newspaper that Maria has run away with …………… .

b …………… hears from Edmund that Julia has eloped with …………… .

c Edmund takes …………… and …………… back to Mansfield Park in a carriage.

d …………… is sorry that she was the one who first introduced Maria to …………… .

e Edmund tells …………… about his last meeting with …………… .

f …………… is ashamed of the way he brought up his daughters.

g Julia and …………… get married.

h …………… divorces Maria, but …………… refuses to marry her.

i Maria and …………… go to live in a small house in the country together.

j Edmund stops loving ……………, and realizes that he loves …………… .

WORD WORK

Use the words in the picture to complete the conversation between Maria and Mrs Norris.

Maria: Why am I in **a)** disgrace like this, sent away from Mansfield Park?

Mrs Norris: I'm afraid your father was **b)** .... by your behaviour, my dear Maria.

Maria: What about Julia? After all, she **c)** .... with Yates! That's a bad thing to do!

Mrs Norris: But now she's married to him, and, well, *you* aren't married to anyone.

Maria: Oh, I was pleased that Rushworth wanted a **d)** .... I never liked him. In fact, it was a **e)** .... to know I didn't have to be his wife any more. But Henry–

Mrs Norris: Don't think about him, my dear. Luckily you have me as your companion, to be a **f)** .... to you when you feel sad. I remember how I took care of you and Julia when you were children – ah, those were the days . . .

Maria: Be quiet! I'll go crazy if I have to spend the rest of my life listening to you, Aunt Norris!

GUESS WHAT

What happens after the story ends? Tick the boxes.

a Tom marries Susan in a few years' time. ☐
b Edmund and Fanny have several children, and bring them up well. ☐
c Mary Crawford marries a good-looking army officer. ☐
d Henry loses his fortune and goes to prison. ☐
e Maria elopes with a new lover, and is never heard of again. ☐
f Mrs Norris returns to live quietly at Mansfield Park. ☐

Project A *Character Acrostic*

An acrostic is a poem where the first letters of the lines spell a name when you read them down the page.

1 Complete the acrostic about Fanny Price with the words or names from the box.

Edmund wife Henry Crawford William lonely Lady Bertram sensible Aunt Norris noisy duty

Feels .... at Mansfield Park at first,
Always helpful to .... ,
Never forgets her brother .... ,
Not excitable or .... ,
Young but ....

Poor but knows her .... ,
Refuses .... ,
Interested in .... ,
Can't bear her .... ,
Edmund's .... at last.

2 Read and match the sentence parts in this acrostic about Edmund Bertram.

- **a** Enjoys listening ☐
- **b** Different from Tom ☐
- **c** Madly in love with Mary ☐
- **d** Understands his real feelings ☐
- **e** Not interested in ☐
- **f** Determined ☐

- **g** in many ways.
- **h** in the end.
- **i** a high social position.
- **j** to the harp.
- **k** to be ordained.
- **l** for a time.

3 Now choose a different character and write your own acrostic.

Mrs Norris

Mary Crawford

Sir Thomas

Lady Bertram

Julia

Maria

Project B Coming-of-age celebrations

1 Read the text about a coming-of-age celebration, and answer the questions.

- **a** Which country does this happen in?
- **b** What day is it on?
- **c** When was the celebration first started?
- **d** Who can take part?
- **e** What do girls usually wear?
- **f** What happens after the celebration in the town hall?

Seijin shiki is the Japanese celebration which is held every year on Coming-of-Age Day, the second Monday in January. It was started as a Japanese celebration and holiday in 1948, when Coming-of-Age Day was originally held on January 15th. In Japan people become adults once they reach twenty, and the *seijin shiki* is for all those who reach this age during that school year. Although young men usually wear western suits, the custom is for girls to wear a kimono. Girls often have their hair and make-up specially done, too. After the celebration, which is usually held at the nearest town hall, the young adults often meet in groups and go to parties or to restaurants.

2 Use the notes about the coming-of-age celebration below to complete the online magazine article.

What's it called? quinceañero
Where does it happen? Latin America, Hispanic families in other countries
What's it for? to celebrate a girl's fifteenth birthday
What's the celebration like? a wedding
What does the girl wear? a long white or pale-coloured dress
What does she throw? a doll
What does she wear for the first time? high-heeled shoes
Who does she dance with first? her father

FIFTEEN AND COUNTING

When Maria Rodriguez reached her ...., her parents held a coming-of-age party for her called a .... This traditional, day-long celebration is held all over ...., as well as in countries where .... have gone to live, like the USA. It is seen as an important moment in a girl's life, when she enters the world as an adult. Families often spend a lot of money on the celebration, which is more like a .... than just a birthday party. Often the flowers, the food and the drink cost a fortune, and photographers are brought in for the day, at great cost.

There were 250 people – family and friends – at Maria's celebration. Maria wore a $1000 long white .... (although some girls prefer a pale .... one), and she looked like a young woman on her wedding day. For many girls from Latin American families living in the United States, the 15th birthday brings the chance to go out with boys. During the celebration, I watched as Maria, standing with her back turned, threw a small .... over her head into the crowd of her girlfriends. 'It's saying goodbye to being a child, goodbye to girlish games, and hello to boys!' Maria laughed.

Another interesting moment of the day was when Maria put on a pair of .... for the very first time, just before going to the 2.00 p.m. Mass held in her honour at the nearby church. Her flat shoes, part of her life as a child, were taken away.

And then after a meal in a restaurant to which everybody was invited, people drank to Maria's health with champagne, and Maria herself cut the large, beautiful white cake. Soon the dancing began, and as always at these celebrations, Maria danced first with her proud ....

3 These photos are about the Turkish coming-of-age ceremony, called *Sünnet*. Research and write about it. Or research and write about a different coming-of-age ceremony of your choice.

A family event

Traditional costumes

Blessed by a stranger

GRAMMAR CHECK

Present Simple Passive and Past Simple Passive

We use the passive when we are interested in a situation or an action, rather than the person who carries out the action.

Mansfield Park is owned by Sir Thomas Bertram.

We use am/is/are (Present Simple Passive), and was/were (Past Simple Passive) with the past participle form of the verb.

Fanny is invited to live with the Bertram family.

In the 18th century Humphry Repton was paid to design rich people's gardens.

Complete Fanny's letter to a friend with the Present or Past Simple Passive form of the verbs in brackets.

Dear Eliza,

I'm sorry I haven't written for so long. But here's my news – I **a)** am married *(marry) to Edmund Bertram now! He* **b)** .... *(ordain) not long ago and* **c)** .... *(give) the living at Mansfield by his father. That's where we live now. You remember that from the age of nine or ten I* **d)** .... *(take care of) by his family? I think I've loved him ever since. For a while he* **e)** .... *(influence) by another woman, and he* **f)** .... *(persuade) he was in love with her. And I* **g)** .... *(propose to) by someone else, but I didn't accept him. What trouble there's been for the family recently! Edmund's sister Maria* **h)** .... *(marry) to rich Mr Rushworth, but sadly they* **i)** .... *(divorce) now. Edmund's younger sister Julia eloped with a young man called John Yates, but soon they* **j)** .... *(discover), actually married and living together. Luckily, all those problems* **k)** .... *(forget) now, and my dear Edmund and I can look forward to a happy life together.*

With warmest wishes, Fanny

GRAMMAR CHECK

First Conditional

We use the First Conditional for a possible future action which depends on another action.

We use will/'ll/won't in the main clause, and the Present Simple in the if clause.
When the if clause comes at the start of the sentence, we put a comma after it.

If Henry really loves Maria, he will ask her to marry him.

When the if clause comes at the end of the sentence, we don't put a comma before it.

Sir Thomas won't be at all pleased if he finds out about the play.

2 Complete these First Conditional sentences with the verbs in brackets. Use the correct form.

Mrs Norris: 'If Fanny **a**) ..comes... (come) to live at Mansfield, that **b**) .... (help) our sister Frances a lot.'

Mrs Grant: 'If Julia **c**) .... (marry) Henry, she **d**) .... (make) him very happy, I'm sure.'

Fanny: 'I think Edmund **e**) .... (fall) in love with Miss Crawford if he **f**) .... (spend) any more time with her!'

Mary: 'You **g**) .... (have) a much more exciting life, Edmund, if you **h**) .... (go) into the army or navy!'

Yates: 'If Tom **i**) .... (agree), we **j**) .... (be able) to rehearse a play here at Mansfield Park.'

Edmund: 'My mother **k**) .... (not need) Fanny as a companion if Aunt Norris **l**) .... (stay) here this evening.'

Sir Thomas: 'I **m**) .... (stop) the wedding if you no longer **n**) .... (wish) to marry Mr Rushworth, Maria!'

Henry: 'If sweet little Fanny **o**) .... (smile) at me, I **p**) .... (be) so happy!'

William: 'If I **q**) .... (not get) a commission, I **r**) .... (not have) a real future in the navy.'

GRAMMAR

GRAMMAR CHECK

Prefixes and suffixes

We use –able/–ed/–d/–ful/–ive to form adjectives.

It is noticeable how talkative the Bertram girls are.

Tom becomes ashamed of his bad behaviour.

Yates thinks the play is going to be successful.

We use –ly/–ily to form adverbs from adjectives.

Sir Thomas generously offers Fanny a home.

Julia happily sees her sister marry Mr Rushworth.

We use un– to form negative adjectives.

Mrs Norris is often unkind to Fanny.

We add –ness to form nouns from adjectives.

Lady Bertram is well known for her laziness.

Complete the text with the words in brackets and prefixes/suffixes from the box. Use some prefixes/suffixes more than once, and make necesssary spelling changes.

–ness –ful –able –ly –ily –ive –ed un– –d

Sir Thomas **a)** ...Kindly... (kind) offers the Mansfield living to Mr Norris. Mrs Norris and her sister, Mrs Price, write **b)** .... (angry) to each other. Mrs Price says that Sir Thomas has an **c)** .... (unnecessary) high opinion of himself! But it is **d)** .... (expense) for her to take care of all her children, so she is **e)** .... (please) when Mrs Norris suggests that young Fanny should live at Mansfield. When Fanny first arrives, she feels **f)** .... (frighten) and **g)** .... (happy). Tom and Edmund are tall young men, while Maria and Julia are **h)** .... (beauty) and sure of themselves. In her **i)** .... (lonely), Fanny often sits crying in a corner. At first, nobody realizes how **j)** .... (misery) she is. But one day, Edmund finds her and asks her **k)** .... (gentle) why she is crying. She feels **l)** .... (embarrass), but his **m)** .... (kind) and **n)** .... (friendly) to her soon make her feel much better.

GRAMMAR CHECK

Used to

We use used to + infinitive when talking about past habits.

Fanny used to miss her family, but soon she felt much happier at Mansfield Park, and didn't think about them so often.

4 Match these sentence halves correctly.

a Sir Thomas used to live alone at Mansfield Park,
b Fanny's father used to be an officer in the navy,
c Maria and Julia used to enjoy themselves while their father was away,
d Mr Rushworth used to think he was in love with Maria,
e Mary Crawford used to like the idea of marrying a baronet,
f Edmund used to take care of Fanny's health,
g The family and servants used to say their prayers in the chapel at Sotherton,
h Henry used to like breaking girls' hearts,
i Mrs Norris used to be proud of her place in the Bertram family,
j Tom used to spend his money on women and the races,

1 but life wasn't so much fun for them when he came home.
2 but his character changed after his illness.
3 but Mr Rushworth's father decided it wasn't necessary.
4 until her behaviour made him think differently.
5 but after Maria's disgrace, she had to leave Mansfield.
6 until he started drinking and no longe[r] went to sea.
7 but he soon began to think more abo[ut] Mary Crawford.
8 until she realized she was falling in love with Edmund.
9 until he married Miss Ward.
10 until he decided he wanted to marry Fanny.

GRAMMAR

GRAMMAR CHECK

Modal auxiliary verbs: Ought to and should

We use ought to or should + infinitive when giving advice about what is the right thing to do.

'You ought to try to be a good son, Tom.'

'You should tell Fanny you love her, Edmund!'

To make a negative, we usually use shouldn't + infinitive.

'You shouldn't spend so much time with Henry, Maria – you're engaged!'

To ask a question, we usually use should.

'Who should I dance with at the ball? William? Henry? Edmund?'

Complete Mrs Norris's advice to Fanny with *should, ought (to)* or *shouldn't.*

a You ..should.. remember your place as a poor cousin.
b You .... expect to ride in a carriage like a fine lady.
c You .... to take more exercise.
d You .... learn to think of your duty to other people.
e You .... to be very grateful to kind Sir Thomas.
f You .... walk, if Miss Crawford is riding your horse.
g You .... sit there dreaming, when there's sewing to be done.
h You .... listen to my advice, and follow it!

Complete Edmund's advice to Fanny about Henry's proposal with *should, ought (to)* or *shouldn't.*

a You ..should.. refuse him if you really can't love him.
b You .... to try to make him a good man.
c You .... remember how much he loves you.
d You .... to think about his proposal carefully.
e You .... make him feel bad about his past behaviour. It isn't right.
f You .... to do what you yourself think is right.

GRAMMAR CHECK

Causative have

We use causative have for describing what someone arranges to be done by someone else.

The Bertrams have some baby clothes sent to Mrs Price.

We use have, the object, and the past participle form of the verb, in that order.

Tom has a stage built in Sir Thomas's library.

Sir Thomas has the carriage brought to the front door.

Mrs Norris has messages taken to the village several times a day.

7 Complete the text with the past participle of the verbs in the box. Use each verb once only.

take	cut	cook	~~clean~~	keep	pay	ride	bring	light	do	put	wash

There are plenty of servants at Mansfield Park to do all the work. The Bertrams have the rooms **a)** cleaned every day, and the fires **b)** .... in winter. They have their meals **c)** .... for them. They also have anything they want **d)** .... to them – they only have to ring for a servant. They have their clothes **e)** .... and **f)** .... in their rooms ready for them to wear in the mornings. Lady Bertram has her hair **g)** .... by a servant, who even helps her to dress. Sir Thomas has his bills **h)** .... and his business papers **i)** .... in order. Outside the house, Sir Thomas has the grass **j)** .... and the gardens **k)** .... care of. He has his horses **l)** .... daily to keep them healthy. But Fanny, as the least important person in the house, has to dress herself and take care of her own clothes.

GRAMMAR

GRAMMAR CHECK

Modal auxiliary verbs: Must/may/can't

We use must + be when we suppose that something is true.

This letter must be from Edmund – I recognize his handwriting!

We use can't + be when we suppose that something is not true.

That can't be Dr Grant's carriage at the door – I can see Henry getting out of it.

We use may + be when we think there is a possibility that something is true, but we are not sure.

That may be a picture of Mr Rushworth, but I don't think it is.

Complete the sentences about the story with *must*, *may* or *can't*.

a That ....must.... be Henry Crawford standing over there – he's talking to a pretty girl as usual!

b Sir Thomas .... be on his way back by now. He's left Antigua and expects to arrive home this week.

c That .... be Maria in the dining room. She's upstairs in her bedroom at the moment.

d I can see a horse disappearing down the road. It .... be Edmund's, but actually I think it looks more like Tom's.

e That .... be Aunt Norris talking to a servant. I recognize her voice.

f Lady Bertram? In the kitchen? It .... be! She never goes there!

g The girl sitting at the table .... be Fanny. She always does her sewing there.

h It's impossible! That .... be Maria in the park, alone with Henry! He isn't her fiancé, Mr Rushworth is!

i Julia .... be happy with Yates – it's hard to tell. She doesn't often write.

j Mary Crawford .... be in London. I saw her in the village half an hour ago!

k Mr Rushworth's mother .... still be alive, but we haven't heard from her or her son for a while.

DOMINOES THE STRUCTURED APPROACH TO READING IN ENGLISH

Dominoes is an enjoyable series of illustrated classic and modern stories in four carefully graded language stages – from Starter to Three – which take learners from beginner to intermediate level.

Each *Domino* reader includes:

- **a good story** to read and enjoy
- **integrated activities** to develop reading skills and increase active vocabulary
- **personalized projects** to make the language and story themes more meaningful
- **seven pages of grammar activities** for consolidation.

Each *Domino* pack contains a reader, plus a MultiROM with:

- **a complete audio recording of the story**, fully dramatized to bring it to life
- **interactive activities** to offer further practice in reading and language skills and to consolidate learning.

If you liked this Level Three *Domino*, why not read these?

The Count of Monte Cristo

Joyce Hannam

'When he went home to Athens, the great prince Theseus left me on the island of Naxos. But why did he leave me? Everyone says that he was tired of me. But when we met, I was the princess of Crete and the most beautiful woman in the Aegean Sea.'

Ariadne's story is one woman's tale of secret love, adventure and of escape – both from danger and from a life that she wanted to leave far behind her – many years ago in Ancient Greece…

Book ISBN: 978 0 19 424819 8
MultiROM Pack ISBN: 978 0 19 424777 1

Dian and the Gorillas

Norma Shapiro

Over the years hunters, poachers, and war have killed many of the gorillas of central Africa. But there are still a few hundred living high in the mists of the Virunga Mountains.

When Dian Fossey first saw a family of wild mountain gorillas in the Virungas she knew that she must help these wonderful animals. This true story tells of the twenty years she lived with them, watched them, wrote about them, and protected them. In the end, she gave her life for them.

Book ISBN: 978 0 19 424827 3
MultiROM Pack ISBN: 978 0 19 424785 6

You can find details and a full list of books in the *Dominoes* catalogue and Oxford English Language Teaching Catalogue, and on the website: www.oup.com/elt

Teachers: see www.oup.com/elt for a full range of online support, or consult your local office.

	CEF	Cambridge Exams	IELTS	TOEFL iBT	TOEIC
Starter	A1	YLE Movers	–	–	–
Level 1	A1–A2	YLE Flyers/KET	3.0	–	–
Level 2	A2–B1	KET-PET	3.0-4.0	–	–
Level 3	B1	PET	4.0	57-86	550